MIKE McKINLEY
LUKE 1-12 FOR YOU

thegoodbook
COMPANY

Luke 1 – 12 For You
© Michael McKinley/The Good Book Company, 2016

Published by:
The Good Book Company

Tel (US): 866 244 2165
Tel (UK): 0333 123 0880
Email (US): info@thegoodbook.com
Email (UK): info@thegoodbook.co.uk

Websites:
North America: www.thegoodbook.com
UK: www.thegoodbook.co.uk
Australia: www.thegoodbook.com.au
New Zealand: www.thegoodbook.co.nz

Unless indicated, all Scripture references are taken from the HOLY BIBLE, NEW
INTERNATIONAL VERSION. Copyright © 2011 Biblica, Inc.™ Used by permission.

(Hardcover) ISBN: 9781784981099
(Paperback) ISBN: 9781910307786

Design by André Parker

Printed in Turkey

CONTENTS

SERIES PREFACE

Each volume of the *God's Word For You* series takes you to the heart of a book of the Bible, and applies its truths to your heart.

The central aim of each title is to be:

- ■ Bible centered
- ■ Christ glorifying
- ■ Relevantly applied
- ■ Easily readable

You can use *Luke 1 – 12 For You:*

To read. You can simply read from cover to cover, as a book that explains and explores the themes, encouragements and challenges of this part of Scripture.

To feed. You can work through this book as part of your own personal regular devotions, or use it alongside a sermon or Bible-study series at your church. Each chapter is divided into two (or occasionally three) shorter sections, with questions for reflection at the end of each.

To lead. You can use this as a resource to help you teach God's word to others, both in small-group and whole-church settings. You'll find tricky verses or concepts explained using ordinary language, and helpful themes and illustrations along with suggested applications.

These books are not commentaries. They assume no understanding of the original Bible languages, nor a high level of biblical knowledge. Verse references are marked in **bold** so that you can refer to them easily. Any words that are used rarely or differently in everyday language outside the church are marked in **gray** when they first appear, and are explained in a glossary toward the back. There, you'll also find details of resources you can use alongside this one, in both personal and church life.

Our prayer is that as you read, you'll be struck not by the contents of this book, but by the book it's helping you open up; and that you'll praise not the author of this book, but the One he is pointing you to.

Carl Laferton, Series Editor

For Dan and Courtney Gifford,
with love and gratitude for a friendship that
can be measured in decades.

Bible translations used:

- NIV: New International Version, 2011 translation (this is the version being quoted unless otherwise stated)
- ESV: English Standard Version

INTRODUCTION TO LUKE 1 – 12

The Gospel of Luke was written to give Christians certainty. That alone makes it a priceless part of Scripture, and a must-read for you and me.

Luke is clear that he was not an eyewitness of the events he describes. This sets him apart from the other **Gospel**† writers; Matthew and John were part of Jesus' inner circle, and reliable tradition holds that Mark's Gospel is the record of Peter's testimony about Jesus. Luke, however, did not come on the scene until the time of the events that he records for us in his "sequel," the book of Acts, where he suddenly begins to write in the first person plural ("we" and "us") about the things that he did as a companion of the **apostle** Paul (see Acts 16:10-17).

Luke's Gospel account is the only one that begins with a personal address. We do not know much about Theophilus, the man to whom Luke addressed both his Gospel (**1:3***) and Acts (see Acts 1:1). Presumably he was both a Christian who had been taught about Jesus (Luke **1:4**) and also wealthy enough to commission Luke to undertake his massive writing project. We barely know more about Luke, and most of what we do know comes from the three brief mentions he received in the letters of Paul. Paul calls him "the doctor" and "our dear friend" in Colossians 4:14. In Philemon v 24 Paul calls him a "fellow worker." At the end of his life Paul mourns those who have abandoned him, saying that, "only Luke is with me" (2 Timothy 4:11).

But Luke's status as an outsider of sorts should not cause us to doubt whether we can trust what he writes. He tells Theophilus (and us) at the outset of his narrative that, having carefully followed these things for quite some time, he has been on a mission to compile an "orderly account" for him (Luke **1:3**) of all "the things that have been fulfilled among us" (**v 1**). Luke expresses no interest in passing on rumors, hearsay, or religious propaganda. He wants his patron

---

† Words in **gray** are defined in the Glossary (page 193).

* All Luke verse references being looked at in each chapter are in **bold**.

to have confidence that he has received an accurate record of what really happened.

But a historian is only as good as his access to the events that really happened, and so it is natural for us to ask whether our guide to the life of Jesus got his information from reputable sources who were really in a position to know the truth. Luke anticipates our concern and identifies his sources as "eyewitnesses and servants of the word" (**v 2**). We know that Luke was with Paul at the time of the apostle's arrest and two-year detention in Jerusalem (Acts 21:17 – 24:27), and it is not unreasonable to speculate this was the period of time when Luke was free to interview these eyewitnesses and gather material for his book.

This explanation of Luke's research methods helps us to understand why it is that there seems to be so much unique material in the first two chapters of his book. Our guide seems to have had special access to the thoughts and feelings of the people that he writes about; he can tell us what Mary felt (Luke 1:29) or what Elizabeth said in the privacy of her room (v 25). While we might be tempted to dismiss those accounts as a writer taking some artistic license with the facts in order to tell a compelling story, Luke insists at the outset that his account is the product of careful research and an orderly passion for the facts. That is why he is able to offer "certainty" (**v 4**).

Major Themes in Luke's Gospel

So, what *are* those things about which we are supposed to have certainty? Here are six recurring, major themes in Luke's Gospel; keep your eye out for them as we go along:

1. *The ministry of the Holy Spirit.* The Spirit gets prominent billing in Luke's sequel, the book of Acts. But Luke's gospel shows us many ways that the third person of the **Trinity** was at work beforehand, preparing us well to see the power of the Spirit unleashed at **Pentecost**. We will see Him at work in the miraculous births of John (1:15) and Jesus (1:35), and in the praises of God's people

in response to those arrivals (e.g. 1:41; 2 v 25-27). The Spirit descends on Jesus at his baptism, empowers him for ministry (4:14, 18) and immediately leads him into the wilderness to be tempted by Satan (4:1). Jesus himself rejoices in the Holy Spirit (10:21) and promises his disciples the presence of the Spirit in their times of need (e.g. 12:12; 24:49).

2. *The importance of prayer.* Luke is quick to highlight Jesus' practice of prayer, especially before important moments (e.g. 9:18, 28). He also records three memorable **parables** that touch on the subject of prayer: the parable about the friend who arrives in the middle of the night (11:5-8), the parable of the persistent woman and the judge (18:1-8), and the parable of the Pharisee and tax collector at prayer in the temple (18:9-14). Luke also shows Jesus repeatedly encouraging his followers to pray (e.g. 6:28) and showing them how to do it (11:2-4).

3. *The joyful praise of God's people.* The first two chapters of Luke read a bit like a Broadway script; people keep interrupting the action by breaking into song! In just chapters 1 and 2, the work of God is greeted with spontaneous words of praise by Mary, Zechariah, the angels, Simeon, and Anna; it is a pattern that continues through the book (e.g. 17:15). Luke uses the verb "rejoice" more than any other author of Scripture.

4. *God's initiative in the salvation of his people.* Luke's account shows that the life and death and resurrection of Jesus are all a part of a definite plan that God has revealed in the Old Testament and is now unfolding for the salvation of his people (e.g. 4:21; 22:37; 24:44). The marvelous triad of parables in chapter 15 gives a vivid picture of what Jesus means when he says that he has come "to seek and save the lost" (19:10). This Gospel is not anything like a self-help manual; it is the story of a divine rescue mission.

5. *Jesus' love for outsiders.* Luke seems particularly concerned that his readers should see that the good news about Jesus is not limited to the people that were valued and honored in the society

of that day. As you go through the book, notice how Luke high-lights the dignity and value of the following groups of people who would not have been valued in that society:

■ Women: Luke's portrait of the role of women in the ministry of Jesus is extraordinary. They are faithful and tenacious friends to Jesus when many of the male disciples abandon him (23:27); they are the special objects of Jesus' mercy and compassion (e.g. 7:11-15); they are avid learners (10:39), financial support-ers (8:3), and models of true sacrificial giving (21:1-4).

■ Children: In ancient times, children were not given the promi-nent place in society that they occupy today. But Luke high-lights Jesus' concern for children who were gravely ill (8:41-42), oppressed by demons (9:42) or even—in the case of the young man from Nain—dead (7:11-15). Each one of these children is said to be an only child, and Jesus' mercy toward both the chil-dren and their parents is palpable in each of Luke's suspense-filled accounts of their healing.

■ Sinners: Some of the most vibrant and memorable characters in Luke's Gospel were some of the most disreputable. Zacchaeus was a notorious crook (19:7), and Luke delicately describes the woman who anointed Jesus' feet with her tears as a woman "who lived a sinful life" (7:37). Each, however, is welcomed by Jesus and praised for their extraordinary love and repentance. Some of Jesus' parables in Luke come to a shocking conclusion, as the sinner (the tax collector, the wastrel son) turns out to be the hero while the upright person (the **Pharisee**, the older brother who stayed home) winds up left out of God's **grace**.

■ Foreigners: While the book of Acts shows the unfolding of God's desire to give his salvation to all the nations, we see glimpses of that plan in Luke's Gospel. The angel declares that the birth of Jesus is good news for the entire earth (2:14), and Simeon says that Jesus will be a light of revelation to the **Gen-tiles** (2:32). Jesus speaks well of Gentiles (4:25-27) and heals the servant of a Roman centurion (7:1-10), marveling that he had not found faith like this among the people of Israel.

6. *The cross and resurrection of Jesus.* This is a bit like saying that Macbeth is a story about a Scottish king, but Luke is obviously concerned that we understand the importance of the cross and resurrection. The other three Gospel writers use the word "salvation" once between them (John 4:22), but Luke uses it repeatedly in his Gospel and in the book of Acts. Luke understands that Jesus' death and resurrection is the only way that we can be saved from the power and penalty of sin (Luke 24:46-47).

If you are reading this book because you are not a follower of Jesus but you want to investigate what he taught and did, then allow me to put all of Luke's cards on the table for you: he wants you to believe in Jesus so that you may be saved from your sins. He wants you to have the same kind of certainty that was available to Theophilus two thousand years ago. Luke has put together a reliable narrative of events that really happened, and so as you read, notice the way that Luke describes events and records details; see if they do not have the ring of eyewitness testimony. Also, let me suggest that you pay careful attention to what kind of person finds a home in the hope that Jesus offers, and what kind of person walks away from Jesus a bit confused about why he isn't impressed with their goodness.

And if you are already a follower of Christ, let me encourage you to read along two lines. First, take notice of what Jesus accomplished through his **incarnation**, ministry, death, and resurrection. Luke uses the word "salvation" and "save" more than any of the other Gospel writers. As you read, look for what the salvation that Jesus brought really means (and what it does not mean). Second, read Luke's Gospel with an eye toward learning more about Jesus' character and priorities. There are obviously some aspects of Jesus' life that we are not meant to emulate (for example, his death on a cross as sacrifice for his people's sins). But both Jesus and his disciples taught that we should look to certain aspects of his character as a model for our own behavior (see 1 John 2:6; 1 Corinthians 11:1): particularly his love (John 13:34), his humility (Philippians 2:3-8), and his sacrificial service to others (Mark 10:42-45). One of the very best ways for believers to grow in Christ-likeness is to spend time learning about and contemplating the story of Jesus as recorded in Luke's faithful narrative.

With those goals in mind, let's turn to that account itself, with the prayer that God would use it to fulfill Luke's intention that we have certainty concerning the things that we have been taught.

1. NOTHING IS IMPOSSIBLE

The first two chapters of Luke, often referred to as the "Infancy Narrative," are particularly memorable for their angelic visitations and vivid accounts of otherwise insignificant people who are swept up in God's great plan of **redemption**. The story begins in the days of Herod, who reigned in Israel under Roman authority from 37 BC to 4 BC. At this point in history, it had been hundreds of years since the Lord had sent a prophet to his people. But that was all about to change, beginning with an elderly Jewish couple that was living with the personal burden of childlessness (**1:5-7**), a socially and economically devastating problem in that society.

John's Arrival

The scene opens on a very unusual day in the life of Zechariah, the husband. A priest, he had been chosen by lot to enter the temple of the Lord and burn incense (**v 8-10**), presumably on the altar that stood in the holy place. In those days, there were more priests than were needed to maintain the functions of the temple, and so many priests went their whole lives without being selected for service. This was literally a once-in-a-lifetime experience for Zechariah, but it turned out not to be the lead story that day, for this was the day that God was beginning to break his silence.

As the priest stood in the temple, a frightening messenger from the Lord appeared at the right side of the altar (**v 11-12**); we find out later that this angel's name is Gabriel (**v 19**). Apparently, Zechariah had been praying at the altar, for after calming him down, Gabriel tells him that his prayer has been heard (**v 13**). At first blush, it seems that Zechariah must have been praying for a child, because the angel indicates that the gift of a son named John is the specific answer to his prayer. But it is hard to imagine that an elderly man with a barren wife (**v 7**) would not have long since given up hope for a child, and Zechariah's **incredulity** at the thought of having a child (**v 18**) makes it seem that the possibility had not entered his mind in quite some time.

If not a child, then what was Zechariah praying for? It seems from Gabriel's description that he might well have been praying for the redemption of Israel. The angel tells Zechariah that John will bring joy and gladness to his childless parents (**v 14**), for reasons we can easily imagine. But he will also cause many to rejoice at his birth, for he will be great before the Lord and will be filled with the Holy Spirit from the womb (**v 15**). Gabriel describes John's future ministry as being one of turning the hearts of Israel to the Lord in the "spirit and power" of **Elijah**, going before the Lord and preparing the people for his arrival (**v 16-17**). By choosing language that clearly echoes the prophecies of **Malachi** (Malachi 3:1; 4:5-6), Gabriel is signaling that the time has come for God to fulfill the promises he had made to Israel some time before.

Zechariah's response is almost comical; a celestial visitor has just met him in the temple and told him that he will have a son who will fulfill an ancient prophecy about Elijah's coming to prepare the way for the Lord, and yet his first thought is about whether or not his elderly wife will be able to get pregnant (Luke **1:18**)! If Zechariah was frightened at Gabriel's first appearance (**v 12**), then the rebuke and reminder of the angel's role and dignity that followed his skepticism (**v 19**) must have completely unnerved him. As a result of his failure to believe this message from the Lord, he is told that he will be silent until all of these events take place (**v 19-23**).

Now, Zechariah's punishment may strike us as unfair. After all, his question does have some merit: how exactly is Elizabeth going to get pregnant? But Gabriel's response shows us that the priest's question wasn't motivated by mere curiosity. Instead, it revealed that he did not believe the angel's words, despite the fact that Gabriel stands in the presence of God and was sent to speak to him (**v 19-20**). God was answering Zechariah's prayers and blessing him beyond all reason, but he lacked the faith to see what was obvious to his wife (compare his reaction to Elizabeth's interpretation of events in **verse 25**). Zechariah was a **righteous** man however, and so the story has a happy ending. After the child was conceived (**v 24**) and born (**v 57**), Zechariah resisted pressure from family members and named the boy John (**v 59-64**) in obedience to the angel's command.

What is clear from this story is that the salvation that John will herald is coming at the initiative and kindness of God. Elizabeth's response in **verse 25** gets right to the **theological** heart of the matter: it is the Lord who has done this, showing favor and taking away her disgrace. The family and neighbors who witness John's birth all recognize it as a gift of God's mercy and share in Elizabeth's joy at what the Lord has done (**v 58**). As a result, the whole region is set atwitter, wondering with awe what exactly God is doing (**v 65-66**) as John appears publicly to Israel in the wilderness.

Jesus' Birth Foretold

There are obvious parallels between the events leading up to the birth of John and those leading up to the birth of Jesus. To name a few, you have:

- the arrival of the angel Gabriel (**v 19, 26-28**).

- the news of a seemingly impossible pregnancy (**v 13, 31**).

- an initial response of fear (**v 12, 29-30**).

- a promise about the child's future and identity (**v 17, 32-33, 35**).

But even with those similarities, it is clear that Mary's child is going to be the greater of the two. Jesus is no mere forerunner for the

Lord, but he is the Son of God himself (**v 35**). He is the one who will receive the throne of the great **King David** (**v 32**), bringing God's never-ending rule to the people of Israel (**v 33**). For this reason, it is fitting that when Elizabeth and Mary met (**v 39-45, 56**), the prophet leapt in his mother's womb for joy and the elderly woman blessed her younger relative.

Perhaps the most striking part of Gabriel's announcement comes in response to Mary's question (**v 34**): how can a virgin have a child? The angel explains to her that she will conceive by the Holy Spirit and the power of the Most High (**v 35**). I'm not sure that that really clarifies matters all that much; in fact, it seems to raise more questions than it answers. But something in the angel's bearing must have told Mary not to ask any more questions, because she let that issue drop there.

The Songs of Praise

The best-known sections of Luke's first chapter are probably the two powerful expressions of praise that accompany the action. In **verses 46-55**, Mary reflects on her visit to Elizabeth in a poem that is often referred to as the Magnificat, after the first word of the poem in the Latin translation. In **verses 67-79**, Zechariah chimes in with a prophecy, referred to as the Benedictus for the same reason. The two songs share some common features:

- Both "singers" understand the birth of their son to be an expression of God's faithfulness to keep his ancient promises to **Abraham** and his descendants (**v 54-55, 70-73**; see Genesis 22:17-18). The Lord had declared that he would send a messenger who would precede his arrival (Malachi 3:1), and Zechariah understands that John is that messenger (Luke **1:76-79**). This section is full of the echoes of Old Testament events.

- Each sees the coming of the **Messiah** as both a victory for the lowly and needy (**v 48-50, 68-69**), and a defeat for the enemies of God's people (**v 51-54, 71, 74**).

■ Zechariah and Mary both express exuberant praise to God for what he is doing. Mary's soul "glorifies"—or "magnifies" (ESV)—the Lord (**v 46**) and her spirit rejoices in him (**v 47**). Usually when we speak of magnifying something, we are making something larger than it really is. But when Mary magnifies the Lord, she isn't making him bigger; she's increasing the love and joy and worship of her heart until it is more in line with how great God is! Zechariah likewise praises the Lord (**v 68**) and exalts his tender mercies (**v 78**).

That's all well and good, but we might well ask: why does Luke interrupt the flow of his story to give us these two poems? They are interesting, but they don't serve to advance the plot at all. Perhaps we can best understand their presence in the text as our author's way of giving us a clue as to how we should read his book. Think about it: here at the outset we have been introduced at length to two characters, Zechariah and Mary. Each comes to understand that God is moving to save his people, and both react with love and praise to the Lord. Might that be a pattern for us to follow as we read Luke's Gospel? We are going to read about things that are even more wonderful than what Mary and Zechariah knew at this point. If they were led to joyfully magnify the Lord, how much more should our hearts convert the fuel of Luke's narrative into flames of praise!

Two "Impossible" Births

Looked at as a whole, Luke 1 tells the story of two impossible births. We are accustomed to stories of women giving birth; according to the best estimates, almost 400,000 babies are born every day. I personally know three families who were blessed with a new baby just this week; births are not particularly extraordinary. But there are two kinds of women who never, ever give birth: very old ladies and virgins. And so it makes sense that both Zechariah and Mary wrestle with the question, "How can this be?"

The answer comes there in **verse 37**, where Gabriel tells Mary that "no word from God will ever fail." Mary does not need to know the mechanics of how it will happen; she only need be confident that the Lord has declared that it will happen. His word never fails. As some older translations render **verse 37**, nothing is impossible with God.

Now, roughly a century ago influential theologians began to doubt whether or not that was actually true. They pointed to the virgin birth of Jesus as a superstition that intelligent, modern people simply couldn't accept. After all, we all know that there is no such thing as a baby being born to a virgin. That's impossible! If Christianity was going to flourish in the **scientific era** (or so the thinking went), it would need to **jettison** these kinds of "myths" that were an insult to our reason and intelligence.

On the surface, that might sound reasonable. But if you look closely, you will see that it does not really do justice to Luke's narrative. Mary and Zechariah and Elizabeth were not gullible bumpkins who didn't know how babies were made and believed fantastical stories (nor, for that matter, were Luke and his original readers). They found the whole idea just as unlikely as you and I might, but that's exactly the point! The great theological truth that Luke is bringing to the forefront by including these events in his "orderly account" is that God's salvation will come in a seemingly impossible way. As Jesus will say later in Luke's Gospel, "What is impossible with man is possible with God" (18:27).

> Mary and Elizabeth were not gullible bumpkins who didn't know how babies were made.

This is not the first time that the Lord has done something like this. Luke's narrative calls to mind a series of extraordinary births in the Old Testament where a promised deliverer is born to an otherwise barren woman (Isaac in Genesis 17 and 21, Samson in Judges 13, Samuel in 1 Samuel 1). The praise of Zechariah and Mary in our passage calls to mind the joyous song of **Hannah** in 1 Samuel 2. In those Old

Testament events, the Lord was establishing a pattern that is brought to fruition in the births of John and Jesus. The point is clear: salvation must come in a way that only God can accomplish so that we will know that God has done it and so that he might get all the glory.

The question that Luke's narrative poses to us as his readers is simply whether or not we will believe that God can do what he says he will do. We must believe that God has accomplished his salvation through the work of Christ. We also must live each day confident that God will keep all of the promises he has made to his people, no matter how far removed they might seem from our daily circumstances. Do we really believe that God will keep us and strengthen us in the darkest of valleys? Or do our feelings and our fears seem more truthful than the words of God? Zechariah's failure to embrace the Lord's promises stands as a warning to us; Mary's humble response (Luke **1:38**) serves as our example. "Blessed is she who has believed that the Lord would fulfill his promises to her" (**v 45**)!

Questions for reflection

1. How do the songs of Mary and Zechariah help you to praise God for his work in human history and in your own life?

2. Why did God use Elizabeth and Mary to achieve his plans to fulfill his promises? How does this resonate in your life, as you consider your own weaknesses and disappointments?

3. When do you find it hardest to believe that God can do what he says he will do? Why do you find that hard? What would it look like to respond in a Mary-like way in those moments?

PART TWO

A Tale of Two Kings

The shadow of **Caesar Augustus** looms large at the beginning of chapter 2. Luke's inclusion of Augustus' name (**2:1**) is not necessary for him to communicate the details regarding when these events took place; his reference to **Quirinius** in **verse 2** actually pinpoints the timing more specifically. The mention of Augustus, however, would have conjured up all of the power and glory of the Roman empire and its authority. He was the most powerful man in the world, flattered by the Roman senate as the "son of a god" and hailed by the poet Virgil as the "son of the Deified, who will make a Golden Age again" (*The Aeneid,* translated A.S. Kline, VI.791-793). At Augustus' instruction, everyone traveled to their ancestral home in order to register (**v 3**).

Observe how these opening verses take us on a downward spiral of power and influence:

■ Augustus (**v 1**), the embodiment of ruthless power and privilege

■ Quirinius (**v 2**), a regional governor

■ Joseph (**v 4**), a poor (but free) man

■ Mary (**v 5**), an unmarried, pregnant woman

■ The baby (**v 6-7**): it would be hard to imagine a less powerful, less privileged person on the planet at that moment than this infant sleeping in a feeding trough for livestock.

Everything in these opening verses points to how lowly the baby was. The irony is palpable for those who know where Luke's narrative is heading; the man recognized by the world as its king (Augustus) lived in a palace surrounded by opulence. This child's beginnings, however, could not have been more humble, but his **kingdom** would far outstrip the glories of Rome. Jesus (as the child is named in **verse 21**, according to the angelic instructions) truly was the Son of the Most High. He would reign on David's throne in an eternal kingdom that puts Augustus' empire to shame (see 1:32-33). The lowly circumstances of Jesus' birth show us that God's kingdom will come in ways that surprise and subvert our expectations about what true greatness and power look like (see 22:25-27).

Evangelicals do not often reflect on the material poverty of Jesus (in comparison to some groups, like the **Franciscans**, who emphasize it). But the fact that the Son of God would enter the world in the most humble way imaginable and then live his life in poverty (8:3) is extremely significant. Consider the words of the apostle Paul, written to the church at Corinth: "For you know the **grace** of our Lord Jesus Christ, that though he was rich, yet for your sake he became poor, so that you through his poverty might become rich" (2 Corinthians 8:9). Jesus became poor so that his people might become spiritually rich through his poverty and suffering.

Before his incarnation, the Son of God was rich beyond anything that Augustus could ever have imagined. But for our sake he stooped to be born not merely as a human (that alone would have been an incredible condescension!), but as a powerless infant in a barn outside an inn in an insignificant town. Because he did, all those who trust in Christ have the sure hope that they will be brought to heaven with Jesus when they die (Luke 23:42-43). Jesus became low in order that we might inherit great spiritual treasure. That is the ultimate point of Luke's **paradoxical** contrast between Caesar Augustus and the baby King Jesus.

Shepherds and Angels

The study in unexpected methods continues when the angel of the Lord appears to the shepherds in the nearby fields (**2:8-9**). A modern publicist might recommend a press conference or a full-page advertisement in the *New York Times*, but the Lord chose to send a messenger to a group of shepherds in the fields. The surprise is lost on those who are used to the role that these men play in the birth narrative, but these would have been among the least likely candidates to receive such an announcement. Shepherds in that society were despised, distrusted and deprived of their civil rights. It is as if God were trying to make it crystal clear to what kind of people the good news of Jesus comes. It does not come to the rich and powerful—those who have no sense of their need. That's not the way that God works. He does not reveal his ways to the Caesars of the world; he is the God who sends a messenger to shepherds.

The shepherds were terrified (**v 9**), as well you might be if your otherwise peaceful night was interrupted by the glory of God shining around you. The angel encouraged them not to be afraid (**v 10**—see 1:13, 30), and informed them of the joyous news of Jesus' birth in Bethlehem. The shepherds could be forgiven if they had trouble reconciling the data: the one who was Savior, Messiah, and Lord (**2:11**) was also a baby lying in a manger (**v 12**). A trip to Bethlehem confirmed all that the Lord has spoken to them through his angel; and as people processed and pondered these events, the news began to spread about the shepherds' story (**v 16-20**).

The events in Bethlehem were meant to inspire praise in those who become aware of them. They were, in the words of the angel, a cause of great joy for the people. The great company of the heavenly host modeled that joy for the shepherds with their declarations of praise (**v 13-14**), and the responses of the humans involved ranged from amazement (those who heard the shepherds' story, **v 18**) to treasuring and pondering these things (Mary, **v 19**) to glorifying and praising God (the shepherds themselves, **v 20**). The surprising news of this section—namely, that God's favor (in the words of the angels in **verse 14**) was resting on people like shepherds, barren women, and poor teenagers—was enough to kindle joy and wonder in those who heard of it. That may be because at the heart of gospel joy are the twin realizations that we are not the kind of people who deserve God's love (in fact, it turns out that there aren't any of that kind of people), but that in his great love God has sent his salvation to people just like us anyway. No wonder Christians have spent the past 2,000 years joining the shepherds in "glorifying and praising God for all the things they [have] heard and seen"!

Simeon's and Anna's Stories

The events recorded in **verses 21-38** (as well as much of the first chapters) may in fact be the testimony of Mary herself. We know from the book of Acts, which Luke also authored, that he probably spent extended time alone in Jerusalem while his traveling companion Paul was in prison (see Acts 21:17 – 24:27). It is not hard to imagine that Mary was herself part of the church family there. This would, of course, explain how Luke had access to the details of Mary's inner life (see Luke **2:19, 33**, 51) and to the two events that took place in the temple shortly after Jesus' birth.

The details of this account show us that Joseph and Mary were obedient, law-keeping Jews. Leviticus 12 prescribed certain rituals for Jews to complete after childbirth, including **circumcising** male infants on the eighth day (Luke **2:21**) and purification rites performed for the mother 33 days later in the temple (**v 22, 24**). In addition, Exodus 13 instructed Israelite parents to set apart their firstborn son to the Lord (Luke **2:23**). After naming the child Jesus in accordance with the angel's instructions (**v 21**), the parents journeyed to Jerusalem in order to fulfill their obligations and sacrifice the pair of birds that were prescribed in the law for poor people.

While in the temple, the family met two extraordinary people. Simeon is described in **verse 25** as righteous and devout. Usually when Luke uses the word "righteous," he is describing someone's conduct toward other people. "Devout" usually has reference to being careful about religious duties. In addition to that, in **verse 25** we are told that the Holy Spirit was on him. The wording there indicates that the Spirit was on him continually and had communicated to Simeon that he would see the Lord's Messiah before he died (**v 26**). When the Spirit brought Simeon into the temple courts, Simeon encountered the family and understood the infant Jesus to be the fulfillment of the Lord's promise to him (**v 27-28**).

At that moment (**v 38**), a widow named Anna came up to the family. A very elderly prophetess, she lived in the temple, where she worshiped, prayed, and fasted constantly (**v 36-37**). In response to the family's presence in the temple, Anna gave thanks to God and began to speak about the child to all who were looking forward to the redemption of Israel (**v 38**).

Both Simeon's and Anna's stories emphasize that the faithful people of Israel were engaged in a long process of waiting for God's act of salvation to come. According to **verse 25**, Simeon was waiting "for the consolation of Israel," a phrase that conjures up Isaiah's prophecies about the arrival of the Lord's comfort and compassion (Isaiah 40:1-2; 49:13). In a similar way, Anna testified to "all who were looking forward to the redemption of Jerusalem" (Luke **2:38**; see Isaiah 52:9). Most likely these crowds thought of the coming redemption in political terms—after all, Israel had been groaning under foreign oppression for centuries. The arrival of a deliverer who would throw off the shackles of Roman rule in Jerusalem and restore the glory of Israel (Luke **2:32**) was certainly a cause for joy and excitement.

But instead of uniting the nation toward a glorious overthrow of Rome, Simeon told Mary that the child was destined actually to be the cause of the falling and rising of many in Israel (**v 34**; see Isaiah 8:14). And as Luke's narrative progresses, we will see that Jesus' ministry effectively splits the nation in two. The Jewish religious establishment, for the most part, will see Jesus as someone to be spoken against (Luke **2:34**), even as many others (including Gentiles, **v 31-32**) receive him as their deliverer.

In addition, something in Simeon's prophecy (**v 34-35**) gives us a clue that the deliverance this child will bring will not come about through political power and military conquest. He tells Mary enigmatically that the coming of this comforter-redeemer means that a sword will pierce her soul; whatever the specific meaning of that phrase, it is clear that being the mother of this child will be a cause of suffering for Mary. And for the first time amid all of the joy in the beginning of Luke's Gospel, we see the cross looming in the distance. This child would indeed redeem Israel, but it would be through pain and cost.

The details of Jesus' salvation are still hazy in these earliest chapters. What is clear, however, is that Jesus is the one sent by God as the redeemer. That is the point that we must see emerging from all of these different stories in the first two chapters of Luke. Simeon had been promised that he would see the Messiah before his death; and when he held the child in his arms, he knew that the promise had been fulfilled (**v 28-29**). Don't miss the power of **verse 30**, where Simeon declares that his eyes have seen God's salvation. God's salvation is not a "what;" it is a "who." To see Jesus is to see God's salvation.

> Christianity is not primarily a code of conduct or philosophy of life; it is a relationship with a Person.

This means that our experience of salvation is not primarily seen in a change of our circumstances or a program of self-improvement, but in a relationship. God did not send us an impersonal force or a guide to better living; he sent us his Son. And so the Christian life is not primarily a code of conduct or a philosophy of life; it is a relationship with a living Person. Our relationship with Jesus displaces everything else to the **periphery** of our lives and becomes the central reality that controls each day. We know God's grace when we look on Jesus with the eyes of faith and say, "This is God's salvation."

Questions for reflection

1. Do you ever envy or fear those in your day who are like Caesar Augustus was in Jesus' day? How does Luke help reorient your perspective?

2. "I bring you good news that will cause great joy" (v 10). Is "joy" your own response to the gospel?

3. "Our relationship with Jesus displaces everything else to the periphery of our lives." How have you experienced this in your life? Are there ways in which it needs to become more true of you?

2. HE WALKED IN OUR SHOES

The first two chapters of Luke are the only access we have to the nature of Jesus' childhood. While we might be tempted to imagine the child Jesus almost like a fully formed adult in a smaller body, the passage before us gives a different picture. Living in his hometown of Nazareth, Jesus obeyed his parents (Luke **2:51**) and grew physically like any normal young person might (**v 40**). He was "filled with wisdom" as a child (**v 39-40**), but also continued to "grow in wisdom" as time passed (**v 52**). And in **verses 41-52**, Luke relates one particular episode from Jesus' early life.

Though we cannot know for certain, it seems reasonable to conclude that knowledge of these events were passed on to him by Mary, who had "treasured all these things in her heart" (**v 51**). Though she did not understand their significance at the time (**v 50**), she must have later come to see the significance of Jesus' **enigmatic** statement in **verse 49**: "Didn't you know I had to be in my Father's house?"

Astonished and Confused

The details of the story might feel familiar even in our day; many parents will know the panic of realizing that a child has gone missing in a crowded place, and the relief of finding him or her unharmed. In this case, the crowds were in Jerusalem for the annual **Passover** festival (**v 41-42**). At the conclusion of the celebration, Mary and Joseph had begun to make their way back north to Nazareth when they realized that Jesus was not among their travelling party (**v 43-44**). After what must have been a harrowing three-day search, they finally found the boy in the temple courts, listening to and questioning the religious scholars who were teaching there (**v 45-46**), apparently oblivious to and uninterested in the frantic search that had been underway.

What follows is a series of astonishments and confusions. Those who heard Jesus were amazed at his understanding of the matters that were being taught (**v 47**). Mary and Joseph were astonished that Jesus would be sitting there, seemingly so indifferent to their distress (**v 48**). In response to Mary's rebuke, the child Jesus seemed genuinely surprised that she and Joseph had not been able to figure out exactly where he would be (**v 49**). And in the end, his parents did not understand what Jesus was talking about (**v 50**).

That this is so is indicated in the interaction between the mother and son in **verses 48-49**. In her rebuke, Mary tells Jesus that his father (meaning Joseph) and she had been searching for him. In response, Jesus seizes on the mention of his earthly and adoptive father in order to remind Mary that his true Father is in heaven. His words are well chosen; Jesus is not an insensitive or thoughtless son. He has actually been in his Father's home doing his Father's will for the entire duration of their search. We see in this interaction that Jesus and Mary are coming to grips with the fact that theirs will not be a normal mother-son relationship. We get a glimpse of Jesus' understanding of his favored relationship with the Father (**v 40, 52**), even as we see that Mary was still wrestling with what this would mean for their earthly family.

> Jesus' identity means that he will always displace things from their "normal" place in our lives.

Our experience of coming to understand Jesus is often a bit like Mary's. Jesus' identity as the Son of God means that he will always displace things from their seemingly "normal" place in our lives. Embracing Jesus as your Savior means that the other relationships in your life (not to mention things like your ambitions, loves, and attitudes toward others) will be rearranged and reconfigured (see Luke 14:26). Everything else in your life needs to accommodate Jesus; if he is the Son of God, it cannot be otherwise.

A Sense of Identity

At first it may seem odd to us that Luke chose to include this story. Roughly twelve years pass in the period described in **2:40**, and another eighteen years will pass between the end of chapter 2 and the beginning of chapter 3. The only indication we have of what was going on during those thirty years of Jesus' life is contained here. Luke clearly must have had a purpose in making room for this particular story in his "orderly account," and so we need to resist the temptation to gloss over this as an interesting but seemingly insignificant story.

Perhaps Luke's purpose is to show us an early glimpse of Jesus' understanding of who he was and what he had come to do. As both the fully divine Son of God and the fully human son of Mary, Jesus was in a unique situation. In this passage, we see a tension arising between the normal obligations of a twelve-year-old boy and the obligations that come to the boy Jesus in his unique role as the Son of God. When those two commitments come into tension, Jesus says that he must obey the will of his heavenly Father (that phrase translated as "be in my Father's house" could also be understood as "be about my Father's business"—see NIV footnote).

Two themes emerge from this account. First, we see clearly that Jesus' sense of his own identity as the Son of God meant that he was obligated to do his Father's will. (Though it is worth noting that Jesus found doing his Father's will to be delightful—see, for instance, John 4:34. We mustn't think that Jesus was normally constrained by the Father's will over and against his own desires.) Jesus' first words in Luke's Gospel tell us that he "had to be" in his Father's house; the Greek word (*dei*) translated there has less a sense of inevitability ("Where else would I be?") and more a sense of necessity ("This was required of me"). Second, we also see that Jesus was passionate about the Scriptures, even as a young man. As he listened and questioned the teachers (Luke **2:46**), his own "understanding and ... answers" surpassed those that could have been expected of someone his age (**v 47**). C.D. Agan asked, and then answered, the question,

> "What does this event reveal of Jesus' character? First, it shows us that he obediently submits to God's purpose for his life ... Second, Jesus' interaction with teachers in the temple shows us that he desired to understand Scripture. He is glad to be in his Father's house, learning more about his Father's purpose, from his Father's word."
>
> (*The Imitation of Christ in the Gospel of Luke*, page 58)

Submitting by Submitting

Jesus' **submission** to his Father's will is a wonderful example to us. Though Jesus' relationship with his Father is unique, those who belong to Jesus become sons and daughters of God in a very real way (Luke 6:36; 11:2). And so if Jesus' status as the Son of God came with a strong awareness of the will of God, it must be that Jesus' followers will share that passion as well. If Jesus was **zealous** to understand the will of God through the word of God, we ought to share that zeal.

It is also significant that Jesus did not use his relationship with the Father as an excuse to rebel against his earthly parents, but instead he was submissive to them (**2:51**). If there was ever a child who could make the case for not listening to his parents, it was Jesus! But when he gently reminds Mary that Joseph is not his father (at least, not in a primary way), he is not using that fact as an excuse to assert his own will. Though he is worthy of all honor and worship, Jesus submitted to the authorities that his Father had placed in his life.

This is an important way that followers of Christ can stand as a witness against the prevailing attitudes of our culture. Respect and submission are not virtues that our wider society values, encourages, or cultivates. Suspicion of authority abounds in our day; if you doubt it, simply look to the chat rooms on the Internet or the talk shows on television. Sometimes this mistrust of those such as politicians, police officers, and parents is well-earned; sadly, authority is often abused in this fallen world. The reality is that many who exercise some kind of power over us will attempt to use it for their own selfish purposes. In addition, the pride in our hearts inclines us to believe that we generally know better than those whom God has placed over us. And so it is no wonder that we chafe and balk at the idea of allowing others to determine what we do.

Remember, though, that the authorities that Jesus submitted to (in this case the authorities were his parents, but see also Luke 20:20-26) were no less sinful and fallible than those in our day. And Jesus actually did always know what is best, unlike you and me. But still he was submissive; he understood that submission to the authorities in his life, limited and fallible though they were, was a way of submitting to his heavenly Father. Surely we must do the same; Christians must understand and speak and live in the knowledge that while authority is often abused in a fallen world, it is fundamentally a gift from God.

Example or Savior?

The problem, of course, is that you and I are not like Jesus. We do not always delight in doing the will of our heavenly Father. We often long to be free from God's will, imagining that we would be happier if we could have our own way. Christians are sometimes the worst offenders when it comes to disrespect for God-given authority. We are happy to obey our leaders in the church (Hebrews 13:17), so long as they don't instruct us to do anything we don't want to do. We respect those who rule over us in government (Romans 13:1), so long as they enact and enforce the policies we advocate. Wives submit to their husbands (Ephesians 5:22-24), so long as they are getting their emotional needs met.

And so Jesus' example helps us by correcting our behavior and demonstrating what we should do, but in the end it condemns us by revealing to us how terribly we have failed to keep God's law. When we see Jesus' example, we see that we are not righteous in and of ourselves; we need a righteousness and obedience that comes from outside of us. So while Luke **2:51** may seem like an insignificant aside, in reality the entirety of our salvation depends on it. If Jesus had not been obedient to his parents, he would not be perfectly holy and could not be a perfect sacrifice for sins (1 Peter 1:18-19). If he were not the obedient child that you and I should have been, he would not possess a righteousness that he is able to give to those who trust in him (Romans 5:19).

The Shadow of the Cross... Already

Readers familiar with Luke's entire narrative can see the shadow of the cross falling across even this seemingly homey little vignette of a family looking for a missing child. Jesus' commitment to his Father's word and his desire to be about his Father's business (Luke **2:49**) would eventually lead him to give up his life.

In the Garden of Gethsemane, we see Jesus' desire for his Father's business come to full fruition. As he contemplated the terrors of the cross there in the garden, Jesus prayed for his Father's will to be done, even if that meant that his own personal will would be frustrated (22:42). Jesus obeyed and submitted himself to the will of his heavenly Father, even when that decision meant that he would go to the cross to suffer and die for the sins of his people. Only in this way could forgiveness be made available to rebellious and disrespectful people. Jesus submitted to the Father's will, and the Father's will was that he should die for all of the ways that his people had sinned against him, including our unrighteous distrust of authority.

Questions for reflection

1. How have you experienced Jesus upsetting what was once "normal" in your own life, as he did in Mary's?

2. How can you live in respect and submission in a counter-cultural way?

3. As you hold your own conduct up against that of Jesus, how does it humble you? How does it make you more grateful for the perfect righteousness that he gives you?

PART TWO

Great and Greater

In chapter 3, Luke returns us to the story of John the Baptist. With a historian's precision, he places John's ministry in the context of both five different Roman officials (**v 1**) and the high priesthood of Caiaphas (**v 2**); the "fifteenth year of the reign of Tiberius Caesar" is most likely AD29. At this time the "word of God came to John ... in the wilderness," just as it did to any number of prophets in the Old Testament (e.g. Jeremiah 1:4; Ezekiel 1:3). In its historical perspective, it is hard to imagine just what John's ministry represented to the people of Israel; after almost 500 years of prophetic silence, the Lord was again speaking through the prophets.

John proclaimed "a baptism of repentance for the forgiveness of sins" (Luke **3:3**). Repentance involves a choice to turn the course of one's life; it involves both turning away from a fundamental commitment to sin and turning toward the Lord in obedience. Luke has already prepared us for the fact that John's ministry would be one of preparation, calling sinners to turn from their ways in light of the Lord's coming (1:16-17, 76-77). Here in **3:4-6**, he brings forward the words of Isaiah the prophet (quoted from Isaiah 40:3-5) to further explain John's ministry in language that calls to mind the preparations that would be made for the arrival of a great ruler. John is the servant who has been dispatched to make the road smooth and level, spiritually speaking, for the coming Lord. His preaching, which seems to have featured confrontational warnings and calls to specific acts of repentance (Luke **3:7-14**), was a proclamation of "good news" (**v 18**) because it was meant to enable people blinded by sin to "see God's salvation" (**v 6**).

John's preaching found a receptive audience (**v 10-11**). Tax collectors and soldiers, two groups not known for their **piety**, were anxious to know his instructions about how to live out repentance in their lives (**v 12-14**—notice that repentance is not going into a different world like a **hermit**, but living in the same world differently!). The crowds were expectant and even began to wonder if the excitement that surrounded John's ministry indicated that he might in fact be the Messiah (**v 15**). But the baptizer would have none of that speculation. He describes Jesus as more honorable than he, so much so that John is "not worthy to untie" his sandals (**v 16**). John's humility is a powerful example to us who would serve Jesus now, whether in a formal ministry capacity or not. Though he was a great man and a mighty prophet (see 7:28), John would not even think of himself as worthy of being the lowest servant of Jesus, but constantly pointed people's attention away from himself and to Jesus.

> John's humility is a powerful example to us who would serve Jesus now.

John tells the crowds that when the "one who is more powerful" comes, he will not baptize with water but "with the Holy Spirit and fire" (**3:16**). **Verse 17** provides a vivid word picture of what that baptism will look like: Jesus is coming to bring the repentant ("the wheat") into the barn, but the unrepentant ("the chaff") will be burned up "with unquenchable fire." In short, the one who is coming will bring a judgment that separates one kind of person from another.

There was, however, one notable exception to the receptivity of the crowds. Luke briefly moves us forward in the story to tell us that Herod the **tetrarch** (also known as Antipas, ruler of the region from about 4 BC to AD 39) eventually took offense at John's rebuke regarding his marriage to his brother's wife and a host of other "evil things he had done." Herod compounded his many offenses by locking the prophet up in prison, thus adding one more wicked deed to the list (**v 19-20**). John's life reminds us that despite moments of popularity, God's servants are normally rejected and despised by those in power (see 13:34). Of course, that pattern will come to a climax in the life and ministry of Jesus—and the fate of the forerunner hints at the fate of the greater One he came to announce.

What's the Genealogy Doing There?

Next, Luke returns us to thoughts of Jesus' earthly family (following on from 2:39-52) in the genealogy that concludes this chapter (**3:23-38**). He traces Jesus' lineage back through Joseph's family, but not without reminding us that Joseph was only thought to be Jesus' father (**v 23**); Luke's readers already know that Mary's son is in reality the son of the Most High (1:32). Readers have long wrestled with the many differences between Jesus' genealogy as it is recorded in Luke and that which opens Matthew's Gospel. The simplest explanation is that in those days there were different methods for describing someone's lineage; while Luke was perhaps sticking with a more strictly biological approach to Jesus' ancestry (with Joseph, the one glaring exception to the biological descent, being noted), Matthew seems to be interested in tracing the royal line of David down into the present through its rightful heirs (for a more detailed discussion, see *The Virgin Birth of Christ* by J. Gresham Machen, page 203).

Like Matthew, Luke highlights Jesus' important ancestors; he indicates in his genealogy that Jesus is the descendant of David (**3:31**—see 1:32) and Abraham (**3:34**—see 1:55). Unlike Matthew, however, he traces the lineage all the way back to Adam, whom he significantly refers to as "the son of God" (**3:38**). Luke seems to be flashing his theological head-lights at us here, wanting to point out that there are actually two people who can truly be spoken of as "the son of God." Both Adam and Jesus have no human, biological father; they own their descent directly to God himself. And so we are meant to see that there's something about the life and ministry of Jesus, the Son of God, that connects into the life and ministry of Adam, the "other" son of God.

Two Other "Sons of God"

The theme of "God's son" is an important thread woven through the storyline of the Bible. When Luke tells us that Adam was the son of God, he is surely referring to Adam's special and direct creation by God; like Jesus, Adam had no biological, earthly father. But the

Genesis narrative also hints at a deeper reality behind Luke's statement that Adam was "the son of God." We are told in the creation account that Adam was created in God's image (Genesis 1:26-27), meaning that he was made with the capacity and desire to reflect the character and purposes of his Creator.

We understand immediately the way in which a child bears the image of his or her parents. I have five children, and while none of them look exactly like their siblings, they all bear some resemblance to me. If we were standing near each other, you wouldn't have trouble believing that they were related to me. But in addition to a physical resemblance, they reflect the priorities and passions of their parents. I don't like camping or the Dallas Cowboys; I love baseball and the music of Johnny Cash. If you met my children, you would see those (impeccable) tastes reflected in their lives. You could learn all kinds of things about me by observing my children.

In a much more profound way Adam, the son of God and the image of God, was created to represent God to the world. But, sadly and shockingly, he was not content with the role that had been granted to him. He rebelled against his Father, and the image of God in mankind was, if not lost altogether, at least significantly defaced. At this point, God would have been justified if he had decided to punish Adam and Eve and entirely abandon the project of creating a race of image-bearers for his glory.

But as the Old Testament drama moves along, we see that God has no such intention. Instead, he calls the nation of Israel out of all the nations on earth to carry forward the mantle that Adam dropped. God identifies Israel as "my son" to Pharaoh (Exodus 4:22-23), delivers them from slavery in Egypt, and then calls them to reflect his image by being holy just as he is holy (Leviticus 11:44-45; 19:2). Ultimately, however, Israel was no more faithful to their charge than Adam was. God's chosen, holy people repeatedly failed to represent the Lord to the nations of the world, and ultimately they were sent into exile. Again, at this point God would have been fully justified if he had decided simply to visit judgment on humanity. But instead he promised yet again that he would not abandon his plan to create a people who would reflect his character and glory (see Jeremiah 31:31-34). During the long period of silence between the prophet Malachi and the arrival of John the Baptist, the people of Israel had only that promise to cling to.

A Question of Identity

Baptism was (and is) an act with layers of deep symbolic significance, and one of the things that it represents is identification with or inclusion in something. So Paul can speak of the Israelites being baptized "into Moses" (1 Corinthians 10:2), and Christians being baptized "into one body" (1 Corinthians 12:13, ESV) and "into Christ" (Romans 6:3; Galatians 3:27). To be baptized is to make a statement about your loyalty, allegiance, and identity. So when Jesus comes to be baptized, he is identifying himself with people who needed "a baptism of repentance for the forgiveness of sins" (Luke **3:3**).

With that context in place, we can understand why Luke puts the record of Jesus' genealogy at the conclusion of his narrative of Jesus' baptism (and, as we will see in the next chapter, immediately before his account of Jesus' temptation in the wilderness). If nothing else, **verses 23-38** represent an unbroken chain of sinful human beings who were in need of repentance. Part of the glory of Jesus' incarnation is that God would willingly stoop into human history, sinful and broken as it is. Jesus' baptism is a powerful picture of that truth, that the sinless Son of God would be willing to identify himself with the sinful sons of God.

What good news then is delivered by the voice from heaven at Jesus' baptism: "You are my Son, whom I love; with you I am well pleased" (**v 22**). This is the son of God, just like Adam and the nation of Israel. This son is loved by God, just like Adam and the nation of Israel. But, unlike Adam and unlike the nation of Israel, this son is perfectly pleasing to his Father! Finally, we have a holy and obedient son of God!

The real surprise of the gospel, of course, is that the pleasing Son did not come into history just to enjoy the love and pleasure of his heavenly Father. Instead, shockingly, we see at his baptism that the sinless Jesus is identifying himself with sinful humanity. He went under the waters of baptism as a way of saying, *Consider me to be one of them.* And ultimately, he became one of us so that he could take our place and take our punishment. The sacrificial kindness of God comes into sharper focus when we see the way that the Father's love and pleasure at Jesus' baptism is replaced by the cup of God's **wrath** at the cross (Luke 22:39-46, see Matthew 27:46). Jesus willingly identified with sinful humanity so that sinful humans could be identified with his righteousness (see 2 Corinthians 5:21).

If your heart grasps the depth of this truth, it will change much about your life. Think about how much time you spend worrying about what others think of you. Look at the way that you respond when you become aware of your failures and shortcomings (either through your own discovery or through the criticism of others). If you are defensive, self-protective, or prone to despair and self-loathing, it is because you desperately want to be perfect, right, and justified; you want to be looked upon and accepted as someone who is lovely and good. The gospel comes to us with a much better salvation than can be found in the fleeting approval of **finite** people. It tells us that in Jesus, we are the righteousness of God and that God (whose opinion truly matters in the end) approves of us 100%, despite our sin. This means that we don't get to boast in our own goodness, but what did that ever do for us in the end? If you understand what it means to have Christ's perfect righteousness as a gift, you will find security and peace and an ever-diminishing concern for the opinions of other people.

> The gospel comes with a much better salvation than can be found in the fleeting approval of finite people.

The Story Isn't Over

All of this means, of course, that the story of God's sons (Adam, Israel, and Jesus) is not over. God's purpose was to create for himself a people, a group of sons and daughters, who would delight in his love and reflect his character and image. Jesus did what both Adam and the nation of Israel failed to do, and now all those who put their trust in him can be called sons and daughters of God (see Hebrews 2:10; Galatians 4:6; 1 John 3:1). In a very real way, the church is called to pick up the mantle of joyfully bearing the image of God and reflecting his character to the world.

Why should Jesus' people love their enemies? Because what we see clearly in the cross of Jesus is that our heavenly Father is a God who loves his enemies; if we would be his children we should exhibit his perfections in our lives (Matthew 5:43-48). Why should followers of Jesus reject sin? Because just as Israel was called to be holy because their God was holy (Leviticus 11:44), so "as obedient children" Christians are called to be holy in all that we do (1 Peter 1:14-16—here, and significantly, Peter quotes Leviticus 11:44).

In this way, we are living out the righteousness of Jesus that is ours as a gift. We are not perfect like Jesus, though God chooses to look at us that way. But as we walk as children of God, we find that the Holy Spirit conforms us more and more to the image of the Son. And we get to have our names added to the genealogy of God's family!

Questions for reflection

1. Do you ever point to yourself, even as you go about obeying Jesus? How? What would pointing only to him, as John the Baptist did, look like?

2. Do you expect to be "rejected and despised by those in power"? Will anticipating or experiencing such rejection keep you quiet, or spur you on?

3. How does knowing you are as loved by the Father as his Son is particularly comfort or liberate you today?

3. TEMPTATION AND LIBERATION (BUT ALSO REJECTION)

With the words "Adam, the son of God" (3:38) ringing in our ears, Luke launches into his account of Jesus' temptation. Three critical pieces of information come our way in **4:1-2**. First, we are told about the involvement of the Holy Spirit in the proceedings. We have already seen the Spirit descend on Jesus at his baptism (3:22), and here in **4:1** Luke summarizes the Spirit's ministry of empowering and guiding Jesus by telling us that Jesus was "full of the Holy Spirit." Jesus was "led by the Spirit" (literally, the Greek text says "led in the Spirit") into his temptation. In order to understand these events properly, we must remember that Jesus' **trials** here (as everywhere in Luke) are part of God's plan and at his initiative. It may seem like Satan unleashed a surprise attack in these verses, but in reality it is the Spirit who has led Jesus out into this conflict.

The second important thing that we are told is that it was the devil who tempted Jesus (**v 2**). We are not introduced to the devil or told anything about him; Luke seems to assume that his readers will be familiar with him. But as we read of the devil tempting the Son of God personally and verbally, Luke likely wants us to be thinking of the temptation of Adam and Eve in the Garden of Eden (see Genesis 3:1-6, where the devil appears in the form of a serpent and suggests that the first humans distrust the word of God).

The third critical piece of information introduced in the opening verses is the duration and location of these events. The hungry Son of

God in the wilderness (Luke **4:1-2**) immediately calls to mind the people of Israel, the earlier "God's son," wandering in the desert, seemingly without adequate food supplies (see Exodus 16:1-3). In Numbers 13 – 14, we read that the Israelite spies spent forty days in the land of in light of the Lord's promise to give them victory over the wicked inhabitants. When the people rebelled by refusing to believe the Lord's promise (Numbers 14:11), the Lord declared that they would wander in the wilderness for forty years, one year for each day the spies had been in the land (v 34). It is therefore highly significant that here in Luke 4, Jesus was hungry in the desert for forty days.

So Luke **4:1-2** helps us to understand what is at stake in the temptation of Jesus. Adam, the son of God (3:38), was tempted by Satan and chose not to obey the word of the Lord. Israel was tested in the wilderness and descended into sinful grumbling and disbelief of God's promises. Now the dramatic tension in this scene is hard to overestimate: will the second Adam succeed where the first one failed? Will the new Israel be faithful where the old one rebelled? Will Satan be able to derail God's cosmic plan to make for himself a people who will love him as holy sons and daughters?

> The dramatic tension is hard to overestimate: will Satan be able to derail God's cosmic plan?

Theologians debate whether or not Jesus was genuinely capable of sin. After all, how could God incarnate give in to sinful temptation? While this is not the place for an in-depth consideration of the issue, it is probably helpful that we remember to understand Jesus' temptation in light of Adam's. That would mean that Jesus would have been able to sin (as a human and like Adam), but because he was the Son of God and was so powerfully led by the Spirit, he did not desire to sin (thus showing himself to be faithful where Adam was not). What must be agreed upon is, first, that Jesus' experience of temptation was real—or else it makes no sense when the writer to the Hebrews tells us that, "We do not have a high priest who is unable to feel sympathy for our weaknesses, but we have one who has been tempted in every way, just as we are—yet he did not sin" (Hebrews 4:15); and second, that he triumphed over temptation so that he could be our Savior.

Temptation #1: Bread into Stones

The first temptation comes in the form of a suggestion that Jesus make some bread for himself in the wilderness (Luke **4:3**). Notice that the devil frames the challenge in light of Jesus' status as God's Son, saying to him, "If you are the Son of God, tell this stone to become bread." The voice from heaven had declared that Jesus was God's Son (3:22); here the devil seems to be asking why God's Son would have to experience this kind of hunger. After all, he possessed the power to make stones into bread if he wanted to (see 3:8).

The nature of this temptation may not be immediately apparent to us. Presumably it would not have been sinful for Jesus to use his powers to feed himself, and as far as we know, he was under no divine restriction against eating. We also know that there was nothing inherently wrong with the making of miraculous bread; Jesus did just that when he fed the multitudes (9:10-17).

What the devil seems to be getting at, though, is not so much about food as it is about trust. Jesus had come in the flesh to identify with humanity so that he could save us. Now the immortal Son of God had taken on flesh with all of its limitations; he now felt exhaustion and hunger and thirst. And so what Satan was tempting him to was something of a way out, as Joel Green outlines:

> "Will Jesus follow the leading of the Spirit and manifest unwavering trust in God to supply his needs, or will he relieve his hunger by exercising his power apart from God? The devil does not deny that he is God's Son, but he *exploits* this status by urging Jesus to use his power in his own way to serve his own ends; he thus

reinterprets 'Son of God' to mean the opposite of faithful obedience and agency on God's behalf."

(The Gospel of Luke, page 194)

Jesus' response helps us to understand the nature of the temptation. His statement, "Man shall not live on bread alone" (**4:4**), is taken from Deuteronomy 8:3. In that passage, the Lord tells Israel that he was both the One who caused them to hunger in the wilderness and the one who provided **manna** to eat. The point of all of this, we read there, is "to teach you that man does not live on bread alone but on every word that comes from the mouth of the Lord." Adam and Eve were tempted to satisfy their hunger by disobeying the word of the Lord (Genesis 3:1-7). Israel was tested in the desert, to see if they would trust the Lord to provide bread to relieve their hunger. But where Adam failed through disobedience and Israel failed through grumbling, Jesus conquered the devil's temptation by choosing faithfulness to God.

Temptation #2: The Authority and Splendor of the World

The second temptation is recorded in Luke **4:5-7**. In it, we see that the devil asserts his right to bestow the authority and splendor of the world's kingdoms to whomever he chooses.

Luke gives no indication that we should be skeptical of this claim. Revelation 13 makes clear that the systems and structures of this fallen world serve the purposes of the devil. In order to receive this gift, however, the devil requires Jesus to bow down and worship him (Luke **4:7**). Now, that temptation might not seem very subtle to us; of course Jesus isn't going to worship the devil. But a closer look reveals that this offer was a **diabolic** attempt to derail the salvation that Jesus had come to accomplish.

In one sense, the devil is offering Jesus something that he has already been promised by his heavenly Father. He will one day surely receive all glory and authority in an eternal kingdom (1:32-33), something doubtlessly greater than whatever the devil could offer him. But Jesus' crown will be so very costly. Jesus' **exaltation** by his heavenly Father will only come after he has (and, we could say, because he has) been crucified (see Philippians 2:8-11).

In essence, what the devil is offering to Jesus is a crown without a cross. The devil will share whatever limited authority and power that God has granted to him, and Jesus can have it without having to suffer. Jesus is being offered the chance to take a kind of glory and authority for himself, but without obeying his Father or saving his people. It is not exaggerating to say that our entire salvation hangs on Jesus' answer in Luke **4:8**.

Again the parallels between the temptation of Jesus and Adam are striking. Both had to choose between obedience to God and the devil's offer of another path to glory. But whereas obedience would have brought Adam incredible blessing, obedience would cost Jesus unimaginable suffering. When Jesus rebuffs the devil and reasserts his desire to be obedient to the word of God, this time quoting from Deuteronomy 6:13, he is committing himself to the path to glory that goes by the way of the cross.

Temptation #3: Throw Yourself Down

In the third temptation (Luke **4:9-11**), it seems that the devil has caught on to Jesus' pattern. If Jesus is going to defeat his attempts at temptation by quoting the Bible, perhaps the way to trip him up is to use the Bible itself in the temptation. The devil takes him up to the highest point of the temple, which was located in the southeastern corner of the temple complex, almost 100 meters above the Kidron Valley below. From there, he instructs Jesus to throw himself down, twisting the promise of divine protection contained in Psalm 91:11-12 as a justification. You can imagine how such a daring feat would have impacted Jesus' ministry; if they saw him jump from the top of the temple, he would have immediately been embraced by the crowds and hailed as the Messiah. It would have proven beyond a shadow of a doubt that God was with him to bless him and his ministry.

But Jesus was not sent to create a sensation by spectacular stunts. He was sent by his Father to proclaim the good news of the kingdom of God (Luke **4:43**) and ultimately to experience rejection by the crowds (**v 28-30**). He corrects the devil's misuse of Scripture, reminding him that the word of God also instructed his people not to test the Lord. It is significant that Deuteronomy 6:16, quoted by Jesus here, refers back to an incident that took place at Massah. There the people of Israel tested the Lord by questioning whether he was with them in the wilderness or not (Exodus 17:7). Now the new Israel is in the wilderness, being tempted to test the Lord by forcing him to prove his care and presence. Yet again, we see that Jesus withstands. He does not cave in; he does not test the Lord to see if he can be trusted.

Until Another Opportunity

The big picture in the temptation narrative is that the pitched battle between Satan and the Son of God has begun in earnest. The first round of the fight goes decisively to Jesus, and the devil retreats with his tail metaphorically tucked between his legs (Luke **4:13**). But an ominous note hangs over the narrative; the devil leaves Jesus "until an opportune time." There will be other skirmishes in this war, not least of which come in the events leading up to the cross. There, we are told explicitly that the devil stands behind Judas' betrayal (22:3) and Peter's denial of Christ (22:31). His influence and activity can also be easily detected in the otherwise inexplicable mockery of the guards (22:63), the anger of the Jewish leaders (23:10-11), and the vitriol of the crowd (23:23). But in an irony that has perhaps become too familiar to us to fully appreciate, it is in that moment of "defeat" that Jesus delivers the decisive blow to his enemy. The battle that rages in the desert in Luke 4 is ultimately won on the cross of **Calvary**.

It is there perhaps that we see how this narrative connects with the daily lives of believers. Too often the temptation of Jesus is reduced to a quarry from which we can mine strategies for resisting temptations ourselves. For example: Jesus quoted the Bible when he was tempted; so should we! So we should, but there is actually much more going on here than that approach admits. Jesus did not stand in the desert primarily as our example; he was there as our Savior.

This section of Luke shows us that Jesus is the Son of God, the new Adam, the new Israel. He stood in the desert and was tempted in our place. Where the other sons of God would not trust the word of the Lord but gave in to diabolic temptation, Jesus was faithful. By virtue of his faithful life and sacrificial death, his people are free from both the power and the penalty of sin (see Romans 6:5-14). His victory in the desert becomes ours, and so we are no longer slaves to sin, unable to resist temptation. We fight against the allure of sin by going to Jesus in faith and prayer, knowing that the One who fought the tempter on our behalf is with us to help us in our time of need.

Questions for reflection

1. The devil offered Jesus "a crown without a cross." Why is this such a powerful temptation—and how does temptation of this form arise in your own life?

2. What does Jesus' resistance teach you about how you can resist temptation?

3. Do you tend to speak to Jesus, your temptation-resisting Savior, when you are undergoing your own temptations? When do you most need to remember to do this?

PART TWO

Setting Free the Oppressed

On the heels of his victory in the wilderness, Jesus returned to his home region of Galilee "in the power of the Spirit" (Luke **4:14**). By all accounts, things were going very well. News about Jesus was spreading "through the whole countryside" (**v 14**), and his teaching in the synagogues was received with praise (**v 15**). Jesus is riding a wave of power and popularity; we might say that things really could not be going better. But the story of Jesus' life and ministry is full of surprising turns, and within a few short verses the adoration of the crowds has given way to thoughts of murder.

At different times in his ministry, Jesus articulated his mission differently. Later on, he will explain his mission in terms of the suffering and rejection that must come to him (see 9:22; 17:25). But when the people of Capernaum wanted him to stay with them, he replied that, "I must proclaim the good news of the **kingdom of God** to the other towns also, because that is why I was sent" (**4:43**). At this point in time, Jesus' mission is to preach his message in Galilee.

It is that "good news of the kingdom of God" that Jesus proclaims in Nazareth, his hometown (2:39). He entered into the synagogue, a place where Jewish men gathered to read, expound, and debate the Scriptures. Given what we have seen in the wilderness about Jesus' love for and use of the Scriptures, it is not surprising that Jesus made it his "custom" to teach in such a context (**4:16**). In this particular gathering the scroll of Isaiah the prophet was given to him to read (**v 16-17**).

It seems that Jesus intentionally unrolled the scroll to a specific place in the text of Isaiah; notice that Luke tells us that Jesus "found the place where it is written…" (**v 17**). While it is almost certain that Jesus would have read a longer section of Isaiah, Luke records for us an excerpt in **verses 18-19** that mostly comes from Isaiah 61:1-2. It is important to compare the two passages:

Isaiah 61:1-2	Luke 4:18-19
The Spirit of the **Sovereign** LORD is on me, because the LORD has anointed me to proclaim good news to the poor.	The Spirit of the Lord is on me, because he has anointed me to proclaim good news to the poor.
He has sent me to bind up the brokenhearted, to proclaim freedom for the captives and release from darkness for the prisoners,	He has sent me to proclaim freedom for the prisoners and recovery of sight for the blind, to set the oppressed free,
to proclaim the year of the LORD's favor	to proclaim the year of the Lord's favor.
and the day of **vengeance** of our God, to comfort all who mourn...	

There are a few changes to the text as Luke records it. First, the language "to set the oppressed free" has been imported into the passage, probably from Isaiah 58:6. This seems to be, in Green's words, an effort to...

> "draw special attention to the word 'release' as a characteristic activity of Jesus' ministry." (*The Gospel of Luke*, page 210)

The second difference is located in Jesus' choice to end his citation of Isaiah before the phrase "the day of vengeance of our God." As Beale and Carson point out, this serves to keep the spotlight on the message of "the Lord's favor" rather than his judgment (*Commentary on the New Testament Use of the Old Testament*, page 289).

In essence, the good news of the kingdom is that the "outsiders"— the poor, the oppressed, the imprisoned and the crippled—have been sent a Spirit-anointed messenger of God's grace. Those who seem to have been beyond the reach of the "Lord's favor" are now recipients of his salvation. Of course, this is no surprise to Luke's readers; we have already been prepared for this reversal of fortune by Mary's reflection on this very theme in her song of praise (Luke 1:46-55, especially verses 50-53).

It is no surprise that the synagogue was fixed on Jesus (**4:20**), waiting to hear what he would say about this important passage. But it is unlikely that they were ready for Jesus' brief and pointed sermon on this text—it was being fulfilled that very day (**v 21**) in their presence! Jesus is telling them that he is the prophet (**v 24**) and the Messiah (a title that comes from the Hebrew word translated "anointed" in Isaiah 61:1), who would be sent by the Lord in the power of the Spirit to declare the good news of God's favor.

> The powerful works of Jesus serve as sermon illustrations.

The powerful works of Jesus that conclude this chapter serve almost as sermon illustrations. Although these healings and **exorcisms** probably took place before Jesus' reading in the Nazareth synagogue (which helps us to understand the comments in Luke **4:23**), Luke does not include them until his reader has the theological "hooks" on which to hang the information. That is to say, the Isaiah passage read in Nazareth informs how we interpret events at the end of the chapter. In Capernaum, the anointing of the Spirit was demonstrated in the authority of his teaching (**v 31-32**), his ministry of healing the sick (**v 38-40**) and his power over impure spirits (**v 33-35, 41**). Both the people (**v 36-37**) and the demons (**v 34, 41**) are forced to acknowledge Jesus' power and authority to carry out his mission of good news.

In fact, Jesus' ministry creates such a sensation that it threatens to overwhelm his God-given mission to preach all over the region (**v 43-44**—Luke's reference to Judea here is probably a way of referring to the entire area where Jewish people lived, rather than specifically to the region of Judea. The people of Capernaum try to prevent his departure (**v 42**) and the demons openly declare what Jesus has only been willing to imply up until this point: namely, that he is the Christ. But Jesus could not remain in one town and he would not allow the demons to create a frenzy with information that the crowds were not yet prepared to handle. What is clear from this section of Luke's narrative is that Jesus is the one sent by the Lord both to declare and to implement God's gracious reign. His arrival is good news for the outcast; the oppressed are being set free.

A Prophet Without Honor

The reader would have every reason to expect that Jesus would be warmly received in Nazareth. As a preacher and healer he had gained something like celebrity status; surely his return to his hometown synagogue would create quite a bit of buzz. And so it comes as no surprise that in response to his message of release, favor, and freedom, the people "all spoke well of him and were amazed at the gracious words that came from his lips" (**v 22**).

There is, however, the issue of his origin. How is it that "Joseph's son" (**v 22**) has become such a powerful **rabbi**? Luke has well prepared his reader for the ironic humor here; we know, of course, that Jesus is not really Joseph's son (see 2:49). Jesus' negative response (**4:23-27**) seems out of step with the crowd's words of approval, but he seems to have access to the unspoken thoughts and attitudes of the people. He knows what they "will quote" and "will tell" him, and the picture is not nearly so rosy as it might appear. They want the "physician" to practice his healing arts on those close to him, but to this point he has declined to do the things in his hometown that he had done in Capernaum (**v 23**).

The townspeople's question might seem innocent and understandable, but Jesus sees below the surface a fundamental rejection of his mission and ministry. He has come to bring unmerited "good news to the poor" and "sight for the blind" (**v 18**), but they expect that they have a right to his blessings because they are from his hometown. They recognize that he has power and they marvel at his teaching, but they do not believe in him or his God-given mission. If the people have a proverb for Jesus (**v 23**), he has one for them as well: "No prophet is accepted in his hometown" (**v 24**).

Jesus' mention of incidents from the ministries of Elijah and **Elisha** (1 Kings 17:7-24 and 2 Kings 5:1-19, respectively) serves a dual purpose. On one hand, it brings to mind the fact that these two prophets were rejected and persecuted during the course of their ministries. They were "Exhibits A and B," proving Jesus' point about prophets who were not accepted at home. On the other hand, both men had performed miracles outside of their homeland. Both Elijah and Elisha pointed forward to Jesus by reminding Israel that God shows his favor and mercy to unlikely people—in their case even Gentiles.

The people of Nazareth (rightly) perceive Jesus' rebuke; they are being compared to Israel in the days of the prophets. They are being reminded that the ministry of the Christ is for the humble, poor, and unlikely. Those who respond to the message with fury (Luke **4:28**) and murderous intentions (**v 29**) will have no part of his blessing. In the end, all there is for Jesus to do is to escape the crowd's clutches, by what means we are not told. He "went on his way" (**v 30**) in order to continue walking in obedience to God and living out the mission on which he had been sent.

A Poke in Your Eye

It's easy to read the confrontation in Nazareth as a warning to others. But if you step back and see it as a warning to those who might be tempted to presume upon God's favor, then perhaps it hits closer to home. Jesus' message is radical; he has been sent to the unlikely: the poor, the unimportant, and the outsider. Those who assume that he owes them his favor (people from his hometown, perhaps even some people who are so committed that they will read commentaries on the Bible) will find themselves watching Jesus' back as he walks away from them. Don't miss the opportunity to take stock of your presumptions; commit yourself to coming to Jesus on the basis of his kindness and mercy, and not on the basis of any merit of your own.

Jesus' understanding of his own mission to bring "good news to the poor" must also shape the church's understanding of our mission. It is easy for Christians to become complacent: content to keep the gospel to themselves or to share it only with put-together and presentable sorts of people. But that kind of behavior is a scandalous warping of the mission. Ask yourself: Are there kinds of people who would not feel welcomed in my church? Are there kinds of people that I wouldn't think of inviting over for a meal? Are there kinds of people that I find too messy and inconvenient to share the love of Christ with? Realize that those kinds of people are the people to whom Jesus declared "the Lord's favor." Do they enjoy yours?

Questions for reflection

1. Were you surprised by the response to Jesus in Nazareth? How do you see similar responses to Jesus around you (and perhaps within you) today?

2. What is the "merit of your own" that you are most likely to think of as contributing to your own salvation?

3. Answer the questions of the previous paragraph. To whom is God's Spirit prompting you actively to show favor, in a Christ-like way?

4. DOCTOR JESUS

At the outset of chapter 5, Luke records three separate miracles that go far beyond a mere display of Jesus' supernatural power. A closer look shows that each one provides a deeper insight into Jesus' identity and ministry. Let's consider them in order:

Miracle #1

Jesus had already announced that he was sent to have an **itinerant** preaching ministry in Judea (4:42-44), and chapter 5 opens with a scene of the people thronging to Jesus, "listening to the word of God" (**5:1**) by the Lake of Gennesaret (another name for the Sea of Galilee). When Jesus sees two boats belonging to three local fisher-men (Simon, James, and John, **v 10**), he has Simon put him out from shore so that he can teach the crowd more effectively (**v 2-3**). We are not told much at this point about Jesus' relationship with the three fishermen, but we know that Jesus has been in Simon's house and has even healed his mother-in-law (4:38-39), and that Simon finds it appropriate to refer to him as "master" (**5:5**).

At the conclusion of his teaching, he instructs Simon to go out far-ther and put out his nets again (**v 4**). Simon's frustrated reply (**v 5**) is understandable; these are not mere recreational fishermen! They have just put in a long night of fruitless labor and then cleaned out their empty nets; heading out again into the sea at the wrong time of day must seem like a complete waste of time. But because Jesus says so, Simon is willing to give it a try. The result makes it clear that Jesus has performed a miracle; the catch of fish is so great that the nets almost break (**v 6**) and the boats threaten to sink (**v 7**).

The meaning of this miracle may not be immediately obvious to us, but it is not lost on Simon Peter. On the face of it, his reaction is surprising; we would expect joyful gratitude and enthusiasm. After all, Jesus has just turned a financially devastating night into an unprecedented windfall! But instead, Simon Peter "fell at Jesus' knees" and begged him to "go away" (**v 8**).

Why on earth would Peter (as he is almost always known after this episode, see 6:14) make such a request? The only answer can be that the miracle has made him acutely aware of Jesus' divine holiness. After all, only God himself has such mastery over nature; God alone controls the fish of the sea. As "a sinful man" (**5:8**), Peter is "astonished" (along with his companions and partners) by this revelation of Jesus' nature (**v 9-10**). In coming face to face with the reality that he is in the presence of the Son of God in human flesh, Peter is undone by his sinfulness. Like Adam and Eve hiding from God after their rebellion (Genesis 3:8) or the Israelites trembling at the appearance of the Lord on Mount Sinai (Exodus 19:16), a sinful man like Peter cannot stand to be in the presence of a holy God.

In his masterful book *The Holiness of God*, R.C. Sproul reflects on the meaning of the miraculous catch of fish:

"We notice that Jesus did not lecture Peter about his sins. There was no rebuke, no word of judgment. All Jesus did was to show Peter how to catch fish. But when the Holy is manifest, no words are need to express it. Peter got the message that was impossible to miss. The **transcendent** standard of all righteousness and all purity blazed before his eyes. Like Isaiah before him, Peter was undone." (page 57)

I would suggest, however, that we have still not seen the most surprising part of this story, because Jesus' response is just as unexpected as Peter's. Jesus doesn't argue with Peter's statement of his own sinfulness. He doesn't say, *Peter, don't talk that way. You need to believe in yourself and have confidence in your abilities.* Instead, Jesus simply tells him not to be afraid and commissions him to a new career. Peter will now "fish for people" (Luke **5:10**).

The sense of that phrase is that Peter and his companions (who seem to be included, given their response in **verse 11**), will be engaged in rescuing people from spiritual danger. The word picture Jesus uses is inverted: while fishermen snatch living fish away to their death, Peter and the other disciples will be engaged in snatching spiritually dying people away to life. How amazing it is that Jesus, the holy Son of God, would use sinful people like Peter to help accomplish his saving work in the world!

Miracle #2

We are not told anything significant about the setting of Jesus' next interaction, with a leper (**v 12-14**); only that it took place "in one of the towns" (**v 12**). The Law of Moses provided instructions for dealing with people who suffered from leprosy (especially Leviticus 13 – 14), and the result was that the individual was considered ritually unclean and was required to live in isolation from the life of the community (see Leviticus 13:45-46). Merely entering a house where leprosy had broken out was enough to render an Israelite unclean (14:46), and lepers were required to walk about announcing their wretched condition lest anyone accidentally come into contact with them and risk contracting their uncleanness.

That helps us to understand the tension lying just beneath the surface of this miraculous healing. The leper was taking a risk in coming to Jesus. Doubtless he had grown accustomed to people avoiding him at all costs. He does not question whether Jesus is able to heal him; rather, he is unsure whether Jesus is willing to do so (Luke **5:12**).

You can easily sense his anxiety: will Jesus reject him because he is an unclean outcast? Far from it! While Jesus presumably could have healed the man with a word (as he does in the next miracle that we will consider), Jesus reaches out and touches him (see 7:14; 13:13; 18:15). Imagine the tenderness and care which that gesture would have communicated to a man used to people avoiding him at all costs. Jesus tells the man to be clean, and "immediately the leprosy left him" (**5:13**).

All that is left is to follow the instructions in the law relating to his cleansing, including showing himself to the priest and performing sacrifices (**v 14**). Despite Jesus' instructions that the healed man should not tell anyone except the priest about what had happened, the news about Jesus "spread all the more" (**v 15**). As the crowds continued to flock to him for healing and teaching, Jesus "often withdrew to lonely places and prayed" (**v 16**).

Just as the miraculous catch of fish was more than a display of power, so this healing is about far more than the physical restoration of a man's body. According to the law, leprosy made a person unclean and unable to participate in the religious life of the nation. Even worse, it was a contagious condition; merely touching a leper made a person unclean himself. But here Jesus reverses that dynamic. He touches the leper, and instead of Jesus becoming unclean, the leper becomes clean! Instead of the leper's defilement passing on to Jesus, Jesus' cleanness is conferred on the leper! It is a perfect picture of Christ's redeeming work, as the holy One replaces our spiritual disease (represented by the man's leprosy) with his own spiritual life (see 2 Corinthians 5:21).

Miracle #3

Luke whisks us off to yet another time and place, this time to a home where Jesus was teaching and healing the sick. Jewish religious leaders—specifically "Pharisees and teachers of the law"—had come from "every village of Galilee and from Judea and Jerusalem" (Luke **5:17**), presumably to evaluate the teaching that had created so much excitement. When four unidentified men try to carry in a paralyzed man in order "to lay him before Jesus" (**v 18**), presumably for healing, they find that the task is impossible due to the density of the crowd in the house (**v 19**).

Undeterred, the men carry their friend up onto the roof of the building. Houses in Israel at that time were normally constructed with ladders or stairs leading up to the roof, offering access to fresh air and extra space for daily tasks (see Acts 10:9). After opening some kind of space in the roof tiles, the four men lower the fifth "into the middle of the crowd, right in front of Jesus" (Luke **5:19**).

Yet again, Jesus' response is surprising. We might expect that he would be annoyed by the interruption and presumption of these men (not to mention the roofing materials that must have been raining down on the crowd!). We could even imagine that Jesus might simply heal the man and move on with his teaching. But instead, "when Jesus saw their faith" (**v 20**)—presumably the faith of all five men in Jesus' ability to heal—he told that paralyzed man that his sins were forgiven.

Luke does not make it clear why Jesus chose to address this man in this particular way. After all, no other healing in his ministry makes an explicit connection between a person's condition and their sin (see Luke 13:1-5). Are we to understand that this man's paralysis was somehow connected to sin in his life? It is surely true that all death and disease is connected inevitably to the presence of sin in our **fallen** world (see, for instance, Genesis 3:3 and Romans 8:20-22), but it is also true that some individual suffering is more directly connected to personal sin (see Psalm 32:1-4). We cannot conclude that definitively in this case.

Whatever the case, the Pharisees and teachers of the law understand the implications of Jesus' statement. They know that only God can forgive sins, and so Jesus' words to the paralyzed man essentially amount to **blasphemy** (Luke **5:21**). In their thinking, Jesus has claimed to exercise a privilege that belongs to God alone. In a sense, they are correct: God is the only one who can forgive sin. But if, as Luke has already shown us, Jesus is the divine Son of God in human flesh, then he does indeed have "authority on earth to forgive sins" (**v 24**). When it comes to who he is, Jesus has, in effect, raised the stakes by closing down the options. He is either

> When it comes to who he is, Jesus has raised the stakes by closing down the options.

God, or a blasphemer; either he is the author and bringer of truth, or he is living and proclaiming a total lie.

The problem is that a claim to forgive sins cannot be verified **empirically**; there is no way to evaluate whether or not the paralyzed man has really been forgiven. Jesus knows their thoughts (**v 22**) and he wants the skeptics "to know" for certain that he has the authority to forgive sins (**v 24**), so he gives them a kind proof that they can see by telling the man to "Get up and walk." It is an easier thing for someone to say, "Your sins are forgiven" (**v 23**); it cannot be proven or disproven. But if someone says, "Get up and walk" to a paralyzed man, it will quickly be evident to everyone whether or not they are a fraud. So when Jesus tells the man, "Get up, take your mat and go home" (**v 24**), he is offering proof that his words about the forgiveness of sins are valid as well. The stakes could not have been higher: either Jesus would be proved to be God in human flesh, or he would be shown to be a blasphemer who claimed authority that did not belong to him. When the man stood up and went home (**v 25**), the truth was inescapable: Jesus has the authority that only God has—the authority to forgive people's sins.

The Response

It is tempting to turn Jesus into a one-dimensional figure. If you place a high value on being morally upright and doing what is right, then you might be attracted to the power and holiness of Jesus. If you value compassion and mercy, then you might be compelled by the forgiveness and tenderness of Jesus. But Luke will not let us walk away with anything less than a full-orbed portrait of Jesus, the one whose power and holiness terrified Peter, and whose compassionate touch cleansed the leper, and whose word forgave the sins of the paralytic.

And also Luke also will not let us walk away without seeing how we ought to respond. Jesus is powerful and holy, but that doesn't mean that sinners cannot come to him. In fact, his compassion is such that people flocked to him for his healing touch (**v 15**). He is able to cleanse us and even commission us for service in his kingdom, making unworthy sinners into fishers of men (**v 10**). When we grasp what a privilege it is to be called into his service, then we will be willing to leave "everything and [follow] him" (**v 11**) like those first disciples. Telling others about the salvation of Jesus shouldn't seem unnatural to a heart that has been grasped by Jesus' power and forgiveness. The people in Jesus' day were "filled with awe" and spontaneously "gave praise to God" (**v 26**); let the same be true of us!

Questions for reflection

1. Have you ever experienced what Peter did in verse 8? If not, do you need to reflect more on Jesus' holiness and your own sinfulness?

2. Does the truth that Jesus uses sinful people to accomplish his purposes encourage you, challenge you, or both? What would change if you lived in light of this truth?

3. What difference does it make to the way you look at your day today to know that your greatest need—forgiveness of sins—has, if you are trusting Christ, already been met?

PART TWO

We have already begun to see the way that Jesus' words and ministry tended to polarize people. Crowds were flocking to Jesus and rejoicing in what he was doing; people were even giving up their careers to follow after him. But there are also some notes in a **minor key**: people in Nazareth wanted to throw him off a cliff. The Pharisees and teachers of the law were outraged by his claim to have authority to forgive sins.

That split of opinion is reflected in **5:27-39**. In **verse 30**, we see the religious leaders grumbling at Jesus' disciples. In **verse 33**, we see a challenge to the religious habits of the disciples. In both cases we see that while some people instinctively understood how to respond to Jesus, some people just couldn't see why his coming was good news.

Sick Sinners and the Great Physician

In **verse 27**, Jesus sees a tax collector named Levi (who is referred to as Matthew in Matthew 9:9), sitting at his station. It is not clear whether or not there has been any previous interaction between the two, but when Jesus calls him to follow after him, Levi does the same thing that Simon Peter, James, and John had done. He "got up, left everything and followed him" (Luke **5:28**).

It is easy for modern readers to miss the significance here. For a faithful Jew in those days, it would be hard to imagine a more loathsome and hated person in all of society. Tax collectors were normally Jews who were working for the Roman government, exacting the very taxes from their fellow-countrymen that served to support the forces that occupied their land. They were infamous for their treachery and willingness to collect more than they had a right to (see John the Baptist's admonition in 3:13). Tax collectors were commonly viewed as the ultimate sinners—the enemies of God and his people. Surely these were the kinds of people that the Messiah would oppose and punish when he arrived?

Given all this, imagine everyone's shock when Jesus asked one of these kinds of people to be his follower! What self-respecting rabbi would allow such a person to be part of his inner circle, let alone command him to come after him? But Jesus doesn't seem to care at all about people's opinions of him and his actions; in fact, he attends "a great banquet" (**5:29**) held in his honor by Levi, despite the presence of "a large crowd of tax collectors and others." The Pharisees and the teachers of the law, the representatives of the **religious establishment**, react with frustration. They complain to the disciples (perhaps they lacked the courage to confront Jesus directly), asking, "Why do you eat and drink with tax collectors and sinners?" (**v 30**).

> Jesus doesn't seem to care at all about people's opinions of him and his actions.

Now, if you are familiar with the Gospel accounts of Jesus' life, it is tempting to simply dismiss the Pharisees as the "bad guys" in every story. And while there is truth to that characterization, it is also easy to miss the dynamics of what was taking place. The Pharisees thought of themselves as the "good guys" in the story; they were the people who were concerned to keep the rules and do what good people should do. Just imagine how you would feel if Jesus showed up and started criticizing the church-going people while frequenting parties hosted by sexually immoral drug dealers with terrorist sympathies! My guess is that we might be scandalized just as much as the Pharisees were.

But in **verses 31-32**, Jesus explains his behavior: "It is not the healthy who need a doctor, but those who are ill. I have not come to call the righteous, but sinners to repentance." That's a strong image. When you go to the doctor, you know you are sick and you know you need help. That's the kind of person that Jesus is calling; that's the kind of person who is willing to leave what he has and follow after him. That's the kind of person who winds up as a friend of Jesus—the one who knows he is desperately sick with sin. And the clear implication of Jesus' teaching is that the Pharisees aren't part of the equation. Jesus came to call sinners, not the righteous. That is to say, he did not come for the people like the Pharisees.

We must not force the details of Jesus' statement beyond what he intends to communicate. He clearly is not granting to the Pharisees that they are really righteous before God. A little later in Luke's Gospel, he is going to call them out for their **hypocrisy** and greed and wickedness (see 11:39-44). Instead, we should understand that Jesus is speaking to the Pharisees on the grounds of their own self-perception. They looked down on others and thought of themselves as righteous, and so when the great Physician came to heal the sin-sick, they had no interest in seeking his help.

Time for a Party

In the next episode (**5:33-39**), Luke records another question about Jesus and his disciples. If we are to understand that the setting is still Levi's banquet, it makes sense that questions about the importance of fasting and religious austerity would be raised. The "they" in **verse 33** probably refers to partygoers, and their pointed question pertains to the difference in practice between Jesus' followers and those of both John the Baptist and the Pharisees. Jesus' disciples "go on eating and drinking" while the others "often fast and pray" (see 18:12). If the **piety** of the disciples is a measure of the teacher, then why does Jesus seem unconcerned to encourage strict religious practices among his followers?

Fasting was a sign both of mourning (whether for sin or painful circumstances) and also hopeful dissatisfaction with the present state of things. We have already met Anna, the prophetess who fasted while she was "looking forward to the redemption of Jerusalem"

(2:36-38). John the Baptist's disciples fasted in anticipation of the arrival of the one who was coming (3:16). So in that light, it would not make sense for Jesus' disciples to fast; the one for whom they were longing had arrived (4:21)!

Jesus draws on an Old Testament image to help us understand what he means. He is like a bridegroom (**5:34-35**—this is a common Old Testament description for the relationship between God and his people; for instance, Hosea 2:19-20 and Isaiah 62:5). As long as Jesus is with them, his disciples (the "friends of the bridegroom") should celebrate. Now is not the time for mourning and hopeful anticipation. Fasting *will* be appropriate after Jesus is "taken from them" at his crucifixion and ascension, for at that time Jesus' followers will once again be in a period of anticipation, this time of his return.

Jesus' arrival has changed everything. To illustrate the implications of this truth, Jesus tells them a parable in Luke **5:36** to the effect that nobody cuts a piece of cloth from a new shirt in order to patch up an old shirt. That makes sense; otherwise you would end up with two ruined shirts. In **verses 37-38**, he points out that no one pours new wine into old wineskins. Wineskins were made from animal hides, and when they were new they were very elastic. After they were used for a while, they became brittle. New wine would expand during the process of **fermentation**, and while a new wineskin would be able to stretch to accommodate that growth, an old wineskin would almost certainly burst.

In both cases, Jesus is making a point about his coming. Judaism is the old garment and the old skins. Jesus' coming and his ministry and his followers are the new garment and the new wine and new skins. Jesus hasn't come to patch up the things that were missing in Jewish religion, even the religion of the most **pious** people like the Pharisees. The point that Jesus is making is that his arrival has brought about something new: a new **covenant** (22:20) and a new reason to celebrate like guests at a wedding. The salvation that Jesus has come to bring demands fresh thinking about what it means to live as God's people.

5:39 has presented a challenge for interpreters. Luke is the only Gospel writer who includes this saying, and at first glance it appears to be out of step with the message of the previous verses. In the little parable that Jesus has just told, his ministry is compared to new wine that cannot be contained by old wineskins, but in **verse 39** it seems that it is old wine that is to be preferred. Two understandings suggest themselves. It could be that Jesus is offering an ironic criticism of the Pharisees and their rigid insistence on the religious forms that Jesus was making **obsolete**. In this reading, their love for "old wine" (which normally is the best wine) causes them to miss out on the really marvelous vintage. On the other hand, it could be that Jesus here is shifting his **metaphor**, acknowledging the reality that older wines are normally best. If this is the case, then Jesus is stressing that his coming is the true fulfillment and true meaning of the **old-covenant** religion that the Pharisees claimed to love so much .

Don't Miss the Party

Jesus' willingness to enjoy a party scandalized the people of his day. They seemed to expect that a respected religious teacher should strive to be serious and strict, but Jesus went to parties and ate and drank (see 7:34), and even speaks of himself as a bridegroom at a wedding celebration. But only the people who saw their acute spiritual need could rejoice at the salvation that Jesus was bringing. For others who were quite content with themselves and their religion, this "new wine" was no cause for celebration.

If we would not miss out on Jesus and the joyful celebration that he brings, we must cultivate an awareness of our need for a spiritual physician, for a Savior. Those who are certain of their own health never go to the doctor; only those who feel sin-sick will seek after a cure. Sadly, it is easy even for followers of Jesus to become self-righteous (in some ways self-righteousness is the besetting sin of religious people!), but it has always been the experience of growing Christians that even as they grow in personal holiness, they also become more aware of their sinfulness.

As we see God's perfect standard more clearly, we also see our own sin more clearly. Someone who has experienced the healing power of the great Physician should never descend into a critical and judgmental spirit toward others. Instead, we ought to be regularly amazed by the grace of God toward sin-sick people like us.

William Jay, the nineteenth-century English pastor, paid a visit to his friend John Newton shortly before the latter's death. Newton had been a notorious slave trader as a younger man, but after experiencing God's grace in Christ he became a respected pastor, author, and hymn-writer. Jay described his last visit to Newton's home like this:

"I saw Mr. Newton near the closing scene. He was hardly able to talk; and all I find I had noted down upon my leaving him was this: "My memory is nearly gone, but I remember two things: That I am a great sinner and that Christ is a great Savior."

(Quoted in Jonathan Aitken, *John Newton,* page 347)

It is not the healthy who need a doctor, but those who are ill. The question is not whether Jesus is able to save, but whether we are able truly to confess our need of him.

Questions for reflection

1. Might you be in any danger of thinking of yourself as spiritually healthy, rather than spiritually sick?

2. What does it mean for you right now to leave everything and follow Jesus, as Levi did?

3. What role might fasting play in your own life, now that the bridegroom is no longer with us?

5. LOSING FRIENDS AND INFLUENCING PEOPLE

Jesus has already begun to arouse the suspicion, and even the hostility, of the religious leadership in Galilee (5:21, 30). Now Luke records two incidents where the actions of Jesus and his disciples bring him into further conflict with "the Pharisees and the teachers of the law" (**6:11**).

The first incident takes place on an unspecified **Sabbath** after Jesus' disciples were walking through the grainfields. As someone walking along a trail in modern times might absentmindedly grab a handful of raspberries off a bush, in the same way the disciples were snacking on the kernels of grain in the field. That required them to "pick some heads of grain [and] rub them in their hands" (**v 1**), and although that behavior was sanctioned by the Old Testament law (see Deuteronomy 23:25), the fact that they were doing so on the Sabbath was enough to catch the attention of the Pharisees, who seemed to be looking closely for opportunities to confront or rebuke Jesus (Luke **6:7**). Some of them accused the disciples of "doing what is unlawful on the Sabbath" (**v 2**).

In the second incident (**v 6-11**), the question of what is "lawful" on the Sabbath comes to the forefront. The scene is tense from the outset, with the Pharisees and the teachers of the law "looking for a reason to accuse Jesus" (**v 7**). Jesus, knowing their thoughts (**v 8**), seems to initiate the conflict intentionally in order to provoke a confrontation. Having the man stand in front of the synagogue, Jesus challenges his opponents, "Which is lawful on the Sabbath: to do good or to do evil, to save life or to destroy it?" (**v 9**).

The question of what was lawful on the Sabbath, raised both in **verse 2** and **verse 9**, was not easily answered. The Old Testament did prescribe rest and the cessation of labor (see Exodus 20:8-11) on the last day of the week, but the law did not give many specific examples of what actions constituted labor that was forbidden on the Sabbath. But religious practice does not tolerate such ambiguity gladly, and so the traditions of the Jewish teachers addressed the silence of the law by listing out thirty-nine specific activities forbidden on the Sabbath, four of which the disciples had violated by their actions in the grainfield. And while Jewish custom permitted medical work on the Sabbath in the case of an emergency like childbirth, nothing about the situation of the man with the shriveled hand demanded that it be addressed on the Sabbath.

In order to address the issue of lawfulness, Jesus appeals to an event from the Old Testament where hunger drove David and his men to eat bread that was meant to be consumed only by the priests (Luke **6:3-4**; see 1 Samuel 21:1-6). Jesus puts the Pharisees in a position where they must either condemn David (which would be an unpopular position) or admit that the application of the Law must be tempered by urgent necessity. The point is clear: the law was never intended to keep hungry people from food.

That does not quite explain his actions in the synagogue, however. The man with a shriveled right hand was not in any life-threatening danger. Presumably his hand had been withered for some time; surely there was no reason why he could not wait until the next day to be healed. But Jesus' question in Luke **6:9** appeals beyond the mere details of this situation to a broader question of what constitutes the kind of law-keeping that pleases God. Is the law best kept when someone does what is good and saves on the Sabbath, like Jesus did in the case of this man? Or is the law fulfilled when someone does evil and postpones someone's healing, as the Pharisees were doing with their suspicious attitude? Jesus registers his answer in **verse 10** by healing the man.

Verse 5 makes clear the bigger issue that lies behind these incidents. Jesus (referring to himself here as the Son of Man) explains that he is the Lord of the Sabbath. The word order of the original Greek stresses the word "Lord" in the thought; it is authority over God's Sabbath that is under discussion. As Darrell Bock puts it,

"With the remark, Jesus argues that he is the authoritative representative of the new way … and that he has authority over the understanding and administration of the Sabbath."

(*Luke 1:1–9:50*, page 527)

Because Jesus is the one with authority over the Sabbath, whatever he permits in terms of observing the day is by definition "what is lawful." The Pharisees' angry response in **verse 11** shows that they understand what Jesus is claiming, and they hate it.

The Choosing of the Twelve

At some point in the midst of all of this controversy and opposition, Jesus spent a night praying on an unidentified mountainside (**v 12**), as was his habit (5:16). When morning came, the reason for Jesus' prayer became obvious. He called his circle of disciples to him, and from that group he "chose twelve of them" (**6:13**), designating these twelve as "apostles" or "sent ones."

While the list of the apostles' names (**v 14-16**) does not contain many details about these men, several points are worth noting. First, while no specific comment is made in this passage, later in Luke's Gospel it becomes clear that the number twelve intentionally mirrors the **twelve tribes of Israel** (22:28-30). Second, as we have already seen, this group was not made up of men whose backgrounds and training would make them obvious candidates for the task. It is unlikely that many rabbis in first-century Palestine were intentionally recruiting a band of fishermen and tax collectors to be their inner circle, but Jesus has already told us that he hasn't come for those the world considers righteous and important (5:31-32).

Third, and most significant, is the presence of Judas Iscariot in the group. "Iscariot" most likely indicates that Judas came from the town of Kerioth, which would make him the only non-**Galilean** in the group. But far more important than the meaning of Judas' name is Luke's ominous foreshadowing at the end of **6:16**, which reminds us that this Judas is the one "who became a traitor" (see 22:47-48). Luke has shown us that Jesus chose these twelve men after careful prayer; this was no rash decision, but one made with the guidance of the heavenly Father. Jesus was well aware that Judas would betray him (see John 6:64), and so even here at the outset of his ministry, the cross looms in the distance.

Happy Now or Then?

Jesus' next significant teaching takes place in "a level place." In that place the apostles ("them" in Luke **6:17**), "a large crowd of his disciples," and "a great number of people" from all over the region surrounded Jesus. The presence of people from Tyre and Sidon (**v 17**) likely indicates that there were Gentiles in the crowds, and Luke tells us that all of these various people desired to "hear him"(**v 18**) and also receive relief from their afflictions (**v 18-19**). The power of the Lord continued to be with Jesus so that he could heal and cure the multitudes.

Jesus' teaching in this context presses further the theme of division that we have seen above. Fundamentally, this section of Jesus' so-called "Sermon on the Plain" (it is best to understand this sermon as distinct from the "Sermon on the Mount" in Matthew 5 – 7) is about the distinction between two kinds of people. The first group is "**blessed**"; they identify with the Son of Man (Luke **6:22**) and the ancient prophets, and can anticipate a "great ... reward in heaven" that will more than compensate them for their present sufferings (**v 23**). The second group is the recipient of a declaration of woe (so common in the ministry of the prophets—see, for instance, Isaiah 5:18); they are identified with the false prophets (Luke **6:26**) and have "already received" (**v 24**) all the good that is coming to them.

The structure of the sermon is fairly simple. In **verses 20-22**, Jesus declares four categories of people to be "blessed": the poor, the hungry, those who weep, and those who are insulted and reviled. In **verses 24-26**, woe is declared to four opposite categories of people: the rich, the well-fed, those who laugh, and the highly-regarded. The teaching here is startling and blunt, turning our normal assumptions about life on their heads (see 1:51-53).

Jesus begins by speaking to the poor, declaring them to be blessed because "yours is the kingdom of God" (**6:20**). It is important not to read Jesus' words in a flat sense: surely he is not declaring that every single poor person in the world is the recipient of God's favor, no matter what their character or way of life is. Instead, we should see that a person's economic condition has the potential to help or to hinder them when it comes to having the spiritual characteristics that God values and rewards.

As the New Testament professor Robert Guelich explains,

"The poor in Judaism referred to those in desperate need (socio-economic element) whose helplessness drove them to a dependent relationship with God (religious element) for the supplying of their needs and **vindication**."

(Quoted in Bock, *Luke 1:1–9:50*, page 574)

Jesus calls these kinds of people "poor in spirit" (Matthew 5:3), who can be said to possess the kingdom of God.

The rich, in contrast, have already received their comfort (Luke **6:24**). Though in reality they are every bit as spiritually helpless as the poor, their material wealth can serve to insulate them from the things that would make them aware of their spiritual neediness. As a result, many rich people miss out on the blessings of Jesus' kingdom (18:18-27 provides the best example; though 23:50 points us to one exception). They should expect no further rewards beyond those meager and temporary pleasures that they receive from their earthly wealth. Woe to them!

In **6:21**, Jesus declares that those who hunger now are blessed because they will be satisfied. In contrast, he calls out a woe on those who are well fed now, for they will go hungry (**v 25**). Again, we should not understand Jesus' words simplistically, as if he simply has a preference for people who either don't have enough to eat or who choose not to eat it. Instead, as with the concept of poverty in **verse 20**, hunger has both material and spiritual overtones. Those who lack physical comforts in this life are most likely to turn to God's promise of help. Those who are full are experiencing now all of the comfort they will ever enjoy; they will go hungry on that future day when God finally sets all things right and gives justice to everyone.

> Those who lack physical comforts in this life are most likely to turn to God's promise.

The third pairing considers the state of those who weep now (**v 21**) with those who laugh now (**v 25**). In an unjust and broken world, God's people are often persecuted and alienated. For that reason, there is in the Bible a long tradition of godly sorrow, from the psalms of complaint (e.g. Psalm 88), to the prophet Jeremiah (see Jeremiah 9:1), to the book of Lamentations, the book of the Bible whose very name speaks of grief. And so Jesus pronounces a blessing over those who weep now, whether because they are being persecuted for their godliness (Luke **6:22-23**) or are simply distraught at the wicked state of the world. There will come a day when righteousness is established and God's people will be able to rejoice over the way that things are. Those who are able to delight and laugh in a world of rebellion like this, however, will find themselves weeping in the world to come.

Finally, Jesus proclaims that "you" are blessed when people hate, exclude, insult, and "reject your name as evil" because of him (**v 22**).

Experiencing that kind of persecution puts one in the company of the godly prophets of old, who themselves were despised and killed because of their work for God (**v 23**). Conversely, if "everyone speaks well of you" (**v 26**), you are in the company of the false prophets, whose message of peace and complacency found a warm reception in a world content with its rebellion against God (see Jeremiah 6:14; 2 Timothy 4:3). The favor of man will have to suffice, for such a person will never know the favor of God.

Recalibration Required

Jesus' words here call us to radically recalibrate the way we think about what it means to live well here and now. The default state of the human heart is to treasure whatever comfort, prosperity, and ease is available in this life. But Jesus warns us that those who make themselves at home in this world will face disastrous consequences when the kingdom of God comes in its fullness. Jesus does not imagine a situation where a person can enjoy both the present pleasures of this world and also the joys of the next world. We must choose our allegiance and the location of our ultimate joy.

A Christian reading Jesus' words here should be reminded to examine his or her heart closely. It is easy to grow comfortable in our sin and at ease with the wickedness of the world around us. This world's system has made some of us wealthy and full; there is a very real danger that we might be spiritually anaesthetized by our possessions. Because our stomachs are full, we may not hunger as we should for a different kind of life and a different kind of world. But in the end, this is the only kind of **discipleship** that Jesus is offering. Following after Jesus means that comfort and wealth and ease in this life are no longer our controlling passions.

But this also means that when we find ourselves deeply dissatisfied with this world, there is hope! God has made us a promise that we can cling to when we find ourselves longing to be finally free from the allure of sin, from physical illness, and from the weariness that comes from living in a world in which you are never quite at home. We can rejoice in these sufferings (Luke **6:23**) because Jesus told us to expect them and because he has promised that we will be blessed in the end.

Questions for reflection

1. How might we as Christians use the law, or our own traditions, to limit the need for us to love and serve others?

2. "Jesus does not imagine a situation where a person can enjoy both the present pleasures of this world and also the joys of the next world." How do you respond to that statement? How does it challenge you?

3. Read through verses 20-22. What will you change in your attitude or actions today in order to seek blessing?

PART TWO

How to Identify Tree Types

One of the great dangers in reading a powerful message like that of the Sermon of the Plain is that we might take it as an instruction to launch a program of external behavior modification. In the next verses, as we read Jesus teaching us to turn the other cheek, give away our shirt, and do good to our enemies, we could easily be tempted to aim to "do better at being a Christian." So it is helpful to hear Jesus teaching us about the need for a radical heart transformation before we can genuinely change, as he does at the end of his sermon. In **verses 43-45**, Jesus uses a simple agricultural principle in order to illustrate a powerful spiritual reality.

Many trees look alike and if we were merely to look at the branch structure and the shape of its leaves, it might be difficult to distinguish one type of tree from another. But, Jesus reminds us in **verse 44**, "each tree is recognized by its own fruit." If you see pears, you know that you are not dealing with a thornbush but with a pear tree. If you see grapes, you know that you are not dealing with a greenbrier shrub, but a grapevine.

There is a direct connection between the quality of a tree and the quality of the fruit that it produces (**v 43**). That principle sheds light on a spiritual reality, for just as a tree brings forth fruit that is consistent with its nature, so "a good man brings good things out of the good stored up in his heart, and an evil man brings evil things out of the evil stored up in his heart" (**v 45**). Our external behaviors (the words we speak, our thoughts and attitudes, and our actions) will inevitably manifest the motivations and loves of our heart.

If we take what Jesus is saying seriously, we have a powerful warning that we must carry with us through the rest of the passage. Any attempt to live out the commands that Jesus gives must come from a heart that is captivated by his grace. But too often when we think about growth in holiness, we are content to do what the pastor and author Paul Tripp calls "fruit stapling":

> "If a tree produces bad apples year after year, there is something drastically wrong with its system, down to its very roots. I won't solve the problem by stapling new apples onto the branches. They also will rot because they are not attached to a life-giving root system. And next spring, I will have the same problem again. I will not see a new crop of healthy apples because my solution has not gone to the heart of the problem. If the tree's roots remain unchanged, it will never produce good apples. The point is that, in personal ministry, much of what we do to produce growth and change in ourselves and others is little more than 'fruit stapling.' It attempts to exchange apples for apples without examining the heart, the root behind the behavior."
>
> (*Instruments in the Redeemer's Hands,* page 63)

Two Kinds of Builders

Jesus further sharpens his point in the following passage. What kind of fruit is it that we should be looking for in the life of someone whose heart truly belongs to Jesus? What is the "good" that a faithful person brings out of her heart (**v 45**)? Jesus frames the fruit that we are looking for in terms of the words our mouths speak. Are we then to assume that the fruit of a good heart is merely a confession of faith in Jesus?

Well, it seems that some people in the crowd were apparently calling Jesus "Lord, Lord" (**v 46**). That would seem to indicate that they are "good trees," but true discipleship involves not only verbal approval of Jesus but also practical obedience to his command. The fruit of obedience (and not merely a profession of devotion to Jesus) shows that the heart below the surface is committed to Jesus.

Jesus vividly presses the point home with the story of two men who each build a house. Upon a casual observation, both houses may well have looked very much alike. The only significant difference between these two houses was located down beneath the surface. One house was "well built" on a deep foundation of rock (**v 48**), a time consuming process to be sure, but well worth it when a flood hit and the house survived. This house represents the spiritual safety of the one who, in Jesus' words, "comes to me and hears my words and puts them into practice" (**v 47**). The other house has been put together quickly directly on the ground "without a foundation"; it was utterly devastated the moment that the torrent hit it (**v 49**). This house represents the spiritual danger that looms over anyone who hears Jesus' words and refuses to do them (**v 49**).

The fates of those houses remind us of what is at stake when it comes to the teaching of Jesus, specifically in the Sermon on the Plain. It is possible to be a fake disciple of Christ; it is possible to call him "Lord, Lord" with your mouth without ever really meaning it. You can try to grow pears out of the thornbush of your heart, but it will not work. Your heart will always be betrayed through your words and actions. When the "flood" hits, either in the trials of earthly life or ultimately in the final judgment of the Lord, the truth about your spiritual condition will be made clear.

Love Like Your Father

We turn now to consider what in some ways is the heart of Jesus' message in the Sermon on the Plain. In **verses 20-26** we are prepared to live for future blessings instead of pursuing immediate gratification in this life. At the end of the sermon, in **verses 46-49**, we are warned regarding the importance of obedience to Jesus' commands. In between, in **verses 27-42**, Jesus tells those "who are listening" (**v 27**) what commands exactly they are to obey.

In **verses 27-28**, we read an exhortation to "love your enemies," followed by three more parallel exhortations that serve to illuminate the theme of loving enemies: "do good to those who hate you, bless those who curse you, pray for those who mistreat you." Those four broad calls to counter-intuitive love are followed by four even more surprising examples of what that kind of love might look like when it is put into practice.

The first is contained in **verse 29**, where Jesus says, "If someone slaps you on one cheek, turn to them the other also." Most likely what is in view here is not so much a punch to the jaw but rather, a personal insult delivered in a disrespectful backhand slap. Jesus is enjoining his followers not to fight for their own dignity in such situations, but to remain engaged and even vulnerable to further insults.

The second example of love for enemies is found at the end of **verse 29**: "If someone takes your coat, do not withhold your shirt from them." The sense here is that the disciple is being robbed of his outer garment, but instead of defending himself he is not even to protect himself from having his undergarment taken as well. The sense is very similar to the previous example; personal affronts are to be met with open-heartedness and even generosity.

The third example ("give to everyone who asks you") and the fourth ("if anyone takes what belongs to you, do not demand it back") in **verse 30** are very similar. Those who would love as Christ commands must be ready to be self-sacrificially generous to those who ask for help and also to those who help themselves to their possessions. The scope of these commands is broad; remain generous and vulnerable to "everyone" and "anyone."

There is the question of whether Jesus intended for these commands to be implemented literally. It is unlikely that he did—it is fairly easy to think of scenarios where a literal implementation of these principles would be absurd and displeasing to God. For example, a woman who is being abused by her spouse should not feel constrained to subject herself to that abuse in the name of "turning the other cheek." Or if a heroin addict asks for money to buy more drugs and thus further enslave himself to his addiction, Christ-like love would compel the Christian not to give it to him (even though a literal implementation of Jesus' words would seem to demand that very thing).

Instead, Jesus it seems is speaking in extreme terms in order to make a serious point about the way his followers love. Even in the crucible of insult and wrong, Christian love should be generous, forbearing, patient, and gracious, treating others as we would wish to be treated (**v 31**). But in the rush to think of ways that each one of these commands would apply in certain real-life situations, it is easy to miss the big picture.

The distinctive fruit in the life of a follower of Christ is love for one's enemies (**v 35**). It does not require a transformed heart to "love those who love you" (**v 32**) or to "do good to those who are good to you" (**v 33**). Anyone can lend generously when they expect to be repaid (**v 34**). People with no relationship with God ("sinners") do such things instinctively; that kind of love is relatively cheap. But when someone loves as the Most High loves, they "will be children of the Most High" (**v 35**). This is not meant to indicate that somehow our loving has the power to make us into God's children, but rather, that when we love like God, we demonstrate our identity as children of the Most High. God's love is distinctive in that he pursues and saves and sacrificially gave his Son, not for good people but for his enemies (see Romans 5:6-8).

For the Christian, it is encouraging that the kind of love that Jesus calls us to, a love that is largely foreign to the world, is actually consistent with who we are in Christ. We are not being forced to do something unnatural to us, but we are simply living out the love that we have received by the Father, whose Spirit lives in us. It is an unbounded reservoir from which we can draw, and as a result we are able to love undeserving people with tenacity and joy.

Whose Sin Do You See?

Now Jesus gives us further examples of what it looks like to be his follower: we are not to judge or condemn, but instead we should forgive (Luke **6:37**) and give to others (**v 38**). Again, we cannot understand the point of these commands unless we see them in light of God's character and disposition toward his people. Despite our sin, he has loved and forgiven us; he has graciously declined to judge or forgive us. If that is true, then how can we have a judgmental or critical spirit toward others?

Jesus is not, of course, telling his believers that they should never exercise judgment, even if such a thing were possible. This is not the battle cry of tolerance that many people imagine that it is. There are places in Scripture where Christians are commanded to exercise discernment regarding the behavior and doctrine of others (1 Corinthians 5:1-5, 12; Galatians 1:6-9). So it cannot be that in commanding us, "Do not judge," Jesus intends for his followers never to evaluate ideas or behaviors negatively.

Instead, he is warning his hearers that their gaze should be on their own failures before they ever look to the failures of others. A believer should acknowledge and address the plank of sin in her own eye before attempting to help her brother with the speck of sin in his eye (Luke 6:41-42). If one is blind to his own faults, he will be of no use in leading others to address their faults (**v 39**). Someone who has not acknowledged their own sin can never teach others to acknowledge their sin (**v 40**).

> Our gaze should be on our own failures before we ever look to the failures of others.

Jesus is warning us not to be so blind to our own faults that we are prone to nurture a **censorious** heart or a critical spirit. A Christian should not judge others harshly or relish the opportunity to criticize others and rejoice when he finds faults with them. He must not leap at the chance to point out the mistakes of others or be ungenerous and **inordinately** negative in his judgments of others. In the end, what Jesus is really concerned about is the measure that his followers use to judge other people (**v 38**).

Now, to be clear: this does not mean that Christians should be indifferent to the sins of their brothers and sisters. Jesus assumes that we should remove the speck in our brother's eye (**v 42**)—a passionate commitment to the teaching of Jesus demands that we do so. And in fact, the Bible repeatedly commends rebuke and correction as a way to show love to someone (e.g. Matthew 18:15; Proverbs 28:23). But only someone who has been made merciful and patient by the merciful and patient grace of God is properly positioned to help someone else deal with their sin.

The Heart Window of Judgmentalism

The issue of judgmentalism gives us a window into our hearts. If we are critical of our brothers and sisters, our hearts don't comprehend who God is, who we are, and how he has forgiven us for our sins. That is why those who judge will be judged, those who condemn will be condemned, and those who forgive will be forgiven. Those who are generous and charitable towards others will receive in abundance, a "good measure, pressed down, shaken together and running over" (Luke **6:38**). The measure you use will show the state of your heart. And as a result, it will correspond to the measure God will use to judge you.

Those who are acutely aware of their own sin and God's extravagant mercy will inevitably be merciful and patient themselves. But if your heart is proud and hard and haughty, then it raises the question of whether you have really comprehended the gospel at all. It indicates that you perhaps have never humbled yourself and gone to God for mercy through Christ. And so you stand in grave danger.

All of these instructions and warnings help us to further understand what Jesus meant when he said that he came to call sinners to repentance (5:32). We sometimes act as if Jesus came to make scandalous sinners like Levi into well-behaved religious people like the Pharisees. In our context, we might be tempted to make certain external behaviors (e.g. attendance at certain church programs, a certain kind of personal appearance) the true indicators that someone is a follower of Jesus. But in fact, the mercy that Jesus shows is not meant to lead us merely to clean up our exteriors; it is meant to make us merciful, generous, and tender-hearted. Those things are the good fruit that grows on a tree that has experienced God's grace. If your life does not manifest these qualities, then you must take your judgmental, critical heart to Jesus for forgiveness. You will not be able to staple this fruit onto the branches of your life. Cry out to Jesus for mercy, and then you will be able to show mercy to others.

Questions for reflection

1. How might you be at risk of "fruit-stapling"? What would heart change look like for you?

2. Do you tend to be too quick to judge others, or do you tend to avoid helping them see their sin at all? Why do you have this tendency, do you think?

3. How has reading this section motivated you to love others, and shown you what that needs to look like specifically in your own life?

6. GREAT UNEXPECTATIONS

Jesus was a surprising person to be around. He left religious leaders marveling, his teaching left crowds astonished, and people were constantly left asking why he did the things that he did. And there are times, if we are honest, when Jesus does not meet our expectations. When we meet him in the Bible, he often says things that challenge and even disturb us. When we look at our lives, we often wonder why Jesus is taking us down this particular path. We are by no means the first to experience this. In chapter 7 of Luke's Gospel, we see a prophet and a religious leader wrestling with Jesus' real identity, and Jesus' shocking behavior.

Unexpected Faith

After an extended period of teaching, Jesus entered into his adopted hometown of Capernaum along the Sea of Galilee (**7:1**). There a group of "elders of the Jews" came to him (**v 3**), asking Jesus to heal a centurion's servant, a man "valued highly" who was on the point of death (**v 2**). In the Roman military scheme a centurion was a commander of a unit of roughly a hundred men, and in that role this centurion had become wealthy enough to build a synagogue for the Jewish people in Capernaum (**v 5**) and powerful enough to have Jewish elders willing to help him (**v 3-5**).

On the surface, it would be hard to imagine someone less likely to send people to approach an itinerant Jewish rabbi in order to plead for help on his behalf; but this is clearly no ordinary centurion. He is a humble man, pleading his unworthiness to approach Jesus himself or even have him come under his roof (**v 6-7**). In any event, Luke has already taught us to expect that it is the outsiders and the unlikely who will come to Jesus!

We are not told how this centurion has heard about Jesus or what he understands about Jesus' identity as the Messiah; he simply needs help and believes that Jesus has extraordinary power to save his cherished servant. As a man with authority in the realm of the military, he has a sense of what it means for Jesus to have authority in the spiritual realm. Just as the centurion has soldiers at the ready to do his bidding (**v 8**), in the same way he believes Jesus has authority to accomplish whatever he wishes to do.

When Jesus heard this, he "was amazed at him" for he had "not found such great faith even in Israel" (**v 9**). In response to this faith Jesus healed the servant from a distance, for when the envoys returned home they found that the servant was well (**v 10**). In this brief story we see both Jesus' incredible power and unusual faith from an unlikely source. The significance of this miracle will be seen in a few verses.

Unexpected Power

Not long after the healing of the centurion's servant, Jesus "went to a town called Nain" accompanied by "his disciples and a large crowd" (**v 11**). Nain was a small and otherwise insignificant town located about 25 miles south of Capernaum. Approaching the entrance to the town, Jesus encountered a truly pitiful scene: a widow accompanying the dead body of her only son (**v 12**).

This woman was in dire straits; not only was she enduring the grief of loss, but as a childless widow in that society she would have no one to provide for her needs in her old age. All her hopes and all her security had died with her son. It is no surprise that upon seeing such sadness, Jesus' "heart went out to her" (**v 13**). But not only does Jesus care—Jesus can help, even when faced by death. Jesus' compassion is on display as he tells the woman not to weep, raises her son from

the dead, and returns him to her (**v 14-15**). The people correctly interpret the significance of Jesus' ministry: the arrival of Jesus signals that
"God has come to help his people" (**v 16**).

This is a story of incredible power—power sufficient to raise the
dead—but Luke is remarkably matter-of-fact in the way that he re-
ports it. It seems that we are not supposed to focus too much on
the details of this particular miracle, but instead to see it in light of a
bigger picture. And Luke does intend for us to read this brief story in
connection with the healing of the centurion's servant in the previous
verses. The literary parallels linking the two miracles are significant. In
each story, we see a person in the grip of grief, a beloved person in the
grip of death, a miraculous healing, and a large crowd that observes
the miracle. Luke's reasons for including these stories in his narrative
(beyond demonstrating Jesus' power to raise the dead) become clear
in the passage that follows.

An Unexpected Messiah

News of "all of these things" spread rapidly around the area, eventually reaching John the Baptist (**v 17-18**) and prompting him to send
messengers to Jesus in order to ask him, "Are you the one who is to
come, or should we expect someone else?" (**v 19-20**). The question is
pointed; John wants a straight answer regarding whether or not Jesus
is in fact the "one who is more powerful" who was to come (3:16).
John's doubts about Jesus are surprising in light of his experience at
Jesus' baptism (3:21-22). Why would the report of Jesus' healing ministry give John cause to doubt him?

Luke does not answer that question, but he has given us enough
context to piece together an answer. We know that John was in
prison at the time of these events (3:18-20); that explains why he
had to hear about Jesus' ministry from others. And before his im-
prisonment, John had spoken about the coming of the more powerful one in terms of judgment. Remember that he had promised the
crowds at the Jordan, "He will baptize you with the Holy Spirit and

fire. His **winnowing** fork is in his hand to clear his threshing floor and to gather the wheat into his barn, but he will burn up the chaff with unquenchable fire" (3:16-17).

In that light, it is not difficult to imagine why John was puzzled. He had understood the coming of the Messiah as a time of justice and punishment for sinners. The Messiah was going to purify Israel and re-establish good in the land; to put it starkly, he would burn up the human trash and cut down the religious deadwood (3:9). John's entire ministry was built around this understanding; he had called people to repentance in light of this coming wrath of God (3:7-8).

But instead of bringing fire and wrath, Jesus was seemingly going from two-bit backwater town to two-bit backwater town on a do-good campaign of healing and preaching! In John's understanding, the Messiah wasn't supposed to come and show mercy to Roman army officials. We can understand why this was not an academic question for John as he rotted in Herod's prison. Perhaps he cherished hopes that Jesus would use his extraordinary power to free him from prison. But Jesus showed no inclination to bring the wrath of God to his enemies.

An Unexpected Response

We might imagine that Jesus would reassure John that in fact he was going to bring judgment to the world. But instead "Jesus cured many who had diseases, sicknesses and evil spirits, and gave sight to many who were blind" (**7:21**). It is almost as if Jesus wants to make the point abundantly clear to John's disciples; they should take back to their master a report of what they "have seen and heard," a message of healing for the sick, life for the dead, and good news for the poor (**v 22**).

Jesus' description of his ministry in **verse 22** is a patchwork of quotes from the book of Isaiah that, writes Green,

"is in form a **symphony** of Isaianic echoes and in substance a 'festival of salvation.'" (*The Gospel of Luke*, page 297)

We have seen in a previous passage that Jesus understood that the prophecies of Isaiah were being fulfilled in his ministry (4:17-21). It turns out that the very miracles that made John unsure about Jesus were actually the things that showed that Jesus was the Messiah. John was not wrong on the facts; there will be a time for judgment. But he was wrong about the timing; Jesus is in effect telling him that now is the time for healing and patience and forgiveness and good news.

Jesus did not meet John's expectations of what the Messiah would be like. And as followers of Christ, we must realize that Jesus may not always meet our expectations. He may not do for us what we would want a deliverer to do; he may not take away a difficult situation or heal a broken relationship in the way that we would hope. He may deem it best for his power to be displayed in your weakness rather than in your strength (2 Corinthians 12:9). He may call

> Jesus may deem it best for his power to be displayed in your weakness rather than in your strength.

you to love people that you would rather not love (Luke 6:27-31). Following Jesus means you may get the unexpected, because Jesus does not always go the way we would expect him to go.

Notice also how patient Jesus is. We might expect that he would blast John for his doubt. Instead, he simply points John to himself and informs him that this is exactly what he should be doing. In fact, Jesus finishes his message to John with a promise of blessing for those who are not discouraged by the fact that he does not do things in the way that they might expect. He says, "Blessed is anyone who does not stumble on account of me" (**7:23**).

In reality, things would only get harder for the disciples who were listening to Jesus. The plan of God would only get more confusing and disappointing as the Messiah was crucified at the hands of wicked men. What kind of victory could that possibly be? But his sacrificial death would prove to be Jesus' ultimate triumph; the way of the cross leads to a crown (Philippians 2:8-11).

If we follow this kind of Messiah, there are bound to be some things that don't immediately make sense to us—things that don't seem to go the way we think things should go. And for that reason, Jesus promises that if we are not tripped up by him and his ways, we will be blessed. Following him will be worth it.

Unexpected Greatness

Once John's messengers have left, Jesus turns to the crowd and talks to them about John. He doesn't want anyone to think that just because John isn't clear on this issue, he wasn't a great prophet. Three times Jesus asks them what they went out to see when they went out to John in the wilderness (Luke 3:7). Did they go out to see a trembling weakling, a "reed swayed by the wind" (**7:24**)? Of course not! Did they go to see a child of luxury, "a man dressed in fine clothes" (**v 25**)? No! They went out to see a prophet (**v 26**). The repetitive questioning here might seem a bit badgering or hostile to a modern audience, but in "the Hebrew world, repetition signaled emphasis" (Edwards, *The Gospel According to Luke*, page 221). Jesus simply wants the crowd to really understand who John is in order that they might be able to grasp who Jesus is.

John was in fact "more than a prophet" (**v 26**); he was the long-awaited prophet that would be the forerunner to the Messiah (**v 27**, see Malachi 3:1). In light of that unique role (rather than any extraordinary personal merit on John's part), Jesus declares that "among those born of women there is no one greater than John" (Luke **7:28**). But it is a measure of the greatness of Jesus and his kingdom that even "the one who is least in the kingdom of God is greater than" this exalted prophet (**v 28**). As the last prophet of the old order of things, John is great. But the new order of things **inaugurated** by Jesus, signaled in the very miraculous healings that confused the prophet, is so great that the very least person in his kingdom has more spiritual privileges than John ever had.

Grumpy Children

As always, the revelation of Jesus demands a response. The religious leaders had rejected John's baptism and his message of repentance. In so doing, they rejected Jesus and "God's purpose for themselves" (**v 30**). Like grumpy children who are not satisfied with any games their friends suggest, they rejected both John, the **ascetic** who preached judgment, and also Jesus, who lavished mercy on people and attended their parties (**v 31-34**).

By this point in Luke's narrative we have come to expect that the tax collectors will see truths that the Pharisees do not (remember the party at Levi's house in Luke 5:27-32). And in fact "all the people, even the tax collectors," heard Jesus and, having been baptized by John, they embraced "God's way" (**7:29**) as Jesus had been describing and demonstrating it. Jesus summarizes his point using what was most likely a common proverb in **verse 35**: wisdom is proved right by all her children. The gist of the saying seems to be that Jesus' followers will show that his ways are correct. Wisdom (or "God's way," **v 29**) is proved to be right ("acknowledged … right") by the approval of her children (those who had been baptized by John and had accepted Jesus' words).

Questions for reflection

1. How do you tend to respond when Jesus says or does something that you don't understand, or instinctively disagree with?

2. As a Christian, how does it make you feel that Jesus is describing you in verse 28?

3. Do you know anyone who is determined to be dissatisfied with God's character and work, as the Pharisees were? How might you challenge them in a similar way as Jesus does in verses 33-34?

PART TWO

One of the key features of Luke's Gospel is the role that outcasts, especially women, play in the narrative (see Introduction). And in **8:1-3**, Luke explains that in addition to the twelve disciples, there was with them a group of women "who had been cured of evil spirits and diseases" (**v 2**). This alone is extraordinary, as in that time it was not normal for rabbis to encourage female followers. But it is also worth noting that these women, all of whose names may have been known to Theophilus, came from a wide range of backgrounds. Joanna (**v 3**) was the wife of an official in Herod's court; Mary (**v 2**) was a former **demoniac** who would have been a social outcast because of her affliction. But this diverse group helped to support Jesus and the disciples "out of their own means."

One of the beauties of the gospel is the way that it applies to and attracts a diverse range of people, and the story of the sinful woman at the dinner party continues that pattern of Jesus having significant interactions with unlikely people.

An Uninvited Guest

In contrast to the dinner party at Levi's house (5:29), this story opens with a dinner invitation from a Pharisee (**7:36**). At Levi's house the guests were sinners and the Pharisees were intruders. Here at Simon's house (we learn the host's name in **v 40**) the host is a Pharisee and it is a sinner who intrudes. The uninvited guest is a "woman … who lived a sinful life" (**v 37**). We are not told more about this woman, but some commentators speculate that Luke's vague way of describing her lifestyle indicates that she was engaged in prostitution, and that may indeed be the case.

Whatever the specifics of the woman's situation, it would be hard to overstate the courage it would require for her to enter into the banquet. Indeed, she was probably anticipating a reception much like what is reflected in Simon's disdain for her in **verse 39**. But something about Jesus' teaching and ministry had given her the strength to approach him with tearful faith that she could be forgiven, although her sins were many (**v 47**).

In this story, the conflict between the three main characters centers on greetings. The passionate greeting of the woman is in marked contrast to Simon's neglect—a difference that Jesus points out in **verses 44-46**. In addition, Jesus' willingness to receive the woman scandalizes the Pharisee (**v 39**). It is deeply ironic that such a woman, rather than such a man, is the one who knows how to properly greet Jesus.

The woman's actions in **verse 38** are described in great detail and are open to a wide range of interpretations. But whatever the specifics may be, it is clear from Jesus' response to her that she was deeply moved by the prospect of forgiveness and restoration from Jesus. In fact, it is hard to read this account without being moved by the woman's public weeping; her willingness to dry Jesus' feet with her hair and shower them with kisses demonstrates a deep and heart-felt reverence for Jesus. She shows "great love" (**v 47**); how different from Simon's "bare minimum" approach to hospitality!

The Pharisee's **ambivalence** about Jesus is fully on display in **verse 39**. He has made Jesus the guest of honor at his dinner party and even refers to him as "teacher"(**v 40**). But clearly Simon is not convinced that the hype surrounding Jesus (v 17) is merited. Though he keeps his doubts about Jesus to himself (**v 39**), he cannot reconcile the idea of Jesus as a prophet with his willingness to allow this "kind of woman ... a sinner" to touch him. As a Pharisee, he would have prided himself on being separate from sinful people; the idea that Jesus might know all about her and yet still accept her love had apparently never occurred to him.

Of Debts and Love

We are not told how Jesus knew what Simon was thinking, but he addresses a brief parable to him in **verses 41-42**. With only three characters, the story is not hard to understand. Two men owe money to a moneylender, but neither can repay the loan. The only difference between them is the amount that they owe; one man owes 500 denarii, roughly a year and a half's wages, while the other owes only one tenth that amount. The reasons why the men were in debt are not provided for us, nor are we told anything else about the moneylender's motivation for forgiving the debts.

The little scenario allows Jesus to ask a question that provokes a self-judgment from Simon: which of the two debtors would love their creditor more? The answer is obvious and to his credit Simon does not try to evade it (**v 43**). Jesus then applies the parable to the immediate situation at the dinner party; just as the greater debtor will respond to mercy with greater love, so the greater sinner (in this case, the woman) responds to Jesus' message of grace with greater love than Simon shows.

Jesus makes it clear to his host that he knew exactly who this woman was; she had "many sins" (**v 47**). But those many sins had been forgiven; her extravagant show of love for Jesus was evidence that God's extravagant forgiveness had taken root in her life. On the other hand Simon, as a Pharisee, was most likely characterized by confidence in his own personal righteousness (see 18:11) rather than an awareness of his sinfulness before God. As a result, he was not thrilled by the prospect of having his "debt" forgiven. He loved Jesus little because he had experienced little forgiveness (**7:47**).

> If we would love Christ more, we must cultivate an awareness of how much we have been forgiven.

Jesus' little parable serves to illustrate why the needy and broken received him with such joy (v 16, 29) while the Pharisees remained so frustrated and offended by him. It also presents an essential principle for the Christian today: if we would love Christ more, we must cultivate a greater awareness of how much we have been forgiven. If we would like to see manifested in our lives a passionate love for Jesus of the type that this woman displayed, we must have the same awareness of our deep sinfulness that she had. Love flows from gratitude, and gratitude comes from a sense of need and an inability to meet that need on our own.

For the Love of God

How can we cultivate such awareness and gratitude? The passage under consideration offers little in terms of practical guidance, but certainly it encourages us to self-examination. Are we more aware of our good deeds and moral **rectitude** (as Simon was) than we are of our deep need for forgiveness (like this sinful woman)? Do we think about our righteousness in terms of external compliance with specific rules? Or do we see ourselves falling horribly short of the perfect love of God that we are called to show to the people around us (6:27-36)? When we are weak and fall into sin, does it drive us to Jesus for mercy, or merely into a resolution to try harder and do better next time? The example of the sinful woman encourages us to be aware of our sin, not in order to celebrate it, but in order to celebrate how great the grace and forgiveness of God really are.

If we find our hearts in need of adjustment in this regard, there is no better place to go than to the cross of Jesus. This passage does not mention the cross or Jesus' plan to die for the sins of his people, but there is a question lingering in the background of the story: how can God forgive this sinful woman without himself being unjust (see Romans 3:25)? How can a holy God forgive someone who has committed "many sins"? God's answer to that question comes at the cross, where Christ paid "the debt" for our sins. As Christ bore our sins on the cross, he satisfied God's justice and secured our forgiveness.

And it is at the cross that we see most clearly how terrible our sin is. The twentieth-century English minister, John Stott, captured this idea in a powerful way:

> "Our sin must be extremely horrible. Nothing reveals the gravity of sin like the cross. For ultimately what sent Christ there

was ... our own greed, envy, cowardice, and other sins, and Christ's resolve in love and mercy to bear their judgment and so put them away. It is impossible for us to face Christ's cross with integrity and not feel ashamed of ourselves. Apathy, selfishness, and complacency blossom everywhere in the world except at the cross. There these **noxious** weeds shrivel and die. There they are seen for the tatty, poisonous things they are. For if there was no way by which the righteous God could righteously forgive our unrighteousness, except that he should bear it himself in Christ, it must be serious indeed..." (*The Cross of Christ*, page 85)

The sinful woman at Simon's party could not know how Jesus would secure her forgiveness. She only knew that her debt was great, that she could not pay it back, and that Jesus was able and willing to sponge it away. Imagine how her heart must have sung when she heard Jesus say to her, "Your sins are forgiven" (Luke **7:48**). Jesus made it clear that he knew her shame and sin and yet he loved her anyway. She may well have entered the party fearful, guilty, and condemned. But because she had faith in Jesus and his salvation, she left hearing Jesus' words of peace ringing in her ears (**v 50**). How could she not love him greatly? How can we not also?

Jesus' words of forgiveness sparked a discussion among the other guests about his identity (**v 49**)—something that has already been a prominent theme in this chapter (v 16, 18-20). For the Pharisees, it was obvious that only God can forgive sins (see 5:21), and so any man who claimed to forgive sins was committing blasphemy. Jesus does not back away from his words though; he simply commends the woman for her faith (**7:50**).

Yet again, we see that when Jesus is properly understood, a decision must follow. For those who see their sin and their need of a Savior, an encounter with Jesus is proof that "God has come to help his people" (v 16). Everyone needs to follow him; anyone can follow him—from his chosen apostles (**8:1**) to those who have suffered evil spiritual oppression (**v 2**); from those with nothing but a sinful past

(**7:37**) to those with money to spare (**8:3**). For those who focus on their own righteousness, Jesus will be dismissed as merely "a friend of tax collectors and sinners" (**7:34**). For those who know they need his righteousness, his kingdom message truly is "good news" (**8:1**); and, having been given all they need by Jesus, they happily give all they have to Jesus, and to his people (**v 3**).

Questions for reflection

1. What is your approach to Jesus more like, honestly: Simon's or the woman's? Why?

2. Are you willing to admit your sinfulness, both to yourself and to the Lord?

3. How do you think the woman felt when she heard Jesus' words in verse 48? How do you feel to hear them directed toward you?

7. OF SOILS AND STORMS

Jesus has been going "from one town and village to another, proclaiming the good news of the kingdom of God" (8:1), and large crowds are gathering from these towns to hear his message (**v 4**). That context is important to understanding the so-called, and famous, "Parable of the Sower," for, despite the subject matter of the parable, Jesus is not concerned about agricultural techniques or harvesting strategies. Instead, he is concerned to make the crowds understand that his message demands a response from those who hear it. His warning in **verse 18** is a good summary of the larger point: "Therefore consider carefully how you listen."

Luke has already introduced us to Jesus' use of parables (5:36; 6:39; 7:41-42), but this parable is longer and contains more "moving parts" than most. While the story itself is not complex, the meaning and purpose of the similitude is less clear. Thankfully we are not left to guess, for Jesus complies with the disciples' request for further explanation (**8:9**) and tells us frankly "the meaning of the parable" (**v 11**).

The Sower, the Seed, and the Soils

At the beginning of **verse 5** we are introduced to a sower and his seed. The seed is identified as "the word of God" (**v 11**), and in the immediate context the sower is clearly Jesus, the one who is proclaiming the good news (though through the next centuries his followers will join him in this task of sowing). Just as a farmer will cast his seed broadly in expectation of a harvest, so Jesus is declaring the word of God without a great deal of discrimination.

The sower and the seed remain constant throughout the parable; the main variable is the type of soil on which the seed falls. Therein lies the explanation for why the same seed sown by the same sower can produce a radically different response in people—a phenomenon that Luke has just demonstrated for us in Simon's house (7:44-47). In the parable, as in farming, the fate of the seed depends on the quality of the soil on which it falls.

The first group of seed falls along the path (**8:5**). A well-traveled path in a field would be packed down and hardened; by definition it was the place where nothing would grow. And so instead of finding a reception into soil that had been tilled and prepared, seed that fell on the path would remain on the surface, exposed both to the feet of people walking by and also to birds looking for an easy meal.

In this case the birds represent the devil, who "comes and takes away the word from their hearts" (**v 12**). This first soil describes people who hear the word of Jesus but are hardened to it. It never takes root in their lives but is immediately gone, bearing no fruit. Sadly, both Luke's Gospel and the book of Acts contain no shortage of examples of this kind of soil (e.g. Luke 6:11; Acts 13:44-46).

The second set of seeds fell on "rocky ground" (Luke **8:6**). This time a plant sprung up in the thin layer of topsoil, but was never able to penetrate its roots into the rocky subsoil below. As a result, the plants had no staying power; they "withered because they had no moisture."

Jesus explains that this kind of soil represents people who "believe for a while, but in the time of testing they fall away" (**v 13**). With this type of people, there is apparent spiritual life in response to the proclamation of the word. They receive it with joy (**v 13**) and initially all appears well. But when trials arise in their lives, it becomes apparent that the spiritual life is superficial. Just as the scorching heat of summer comes and tests the depth of a plant's root system, so in the same way the difficulties of life will serve to reveal whether or not the roots of our faith run deep.

In the third type of soil the seed meets with competition. There is something else growing in this field: thornbushes that would rob the seedlings of water, light, and nutrients. Growing up alongside the fruit of the seed, these thorns "choked the plants" (**v 7**).

This kind of soil represents people who "hear, but ... they do not mature" (**v 14**). The new growth of spiritual life finds itself in competition with "life's worries, riches and pleasures." Those worldly concerns

> The difficulties of life will serve to reveal whether or not the roots of our faith run deep.

choke the life out of the plant and prevent the seed from growing into a fruitful plant. Luke shows us an example of this dynamic in the story of the rich ruler who wanted to follow Jesus but was unwilling to leave behind his considerable riches (18:18-24). Many would-be disciples have found themselves walking away from Jesus in order to pursue worldly wealth and the pleasures of this life.

So far the picture is fairly depressing. The message of the kingdom is rejected and abandoned for many different reasons. But when the seed falls "on good soil" (**8:8**), we see a very different result. When the seed meets a "noble and good heart" (**v 15**), defined there by Jesus as a heart that hears the word, retains it, and perseveres in it, the result is an impressive and fruitful crop.

This spectacular growth more than compensates for the disappointment of the other three soils. Reaping a crop "a hundred times more than was sown" represents an extraordinary harvest (**v 8**). Suddenly, what seemed to be an ill-conceived and ineffective sowing strategy turns out to be the power of God at work to produce an astounding result. As Edwards puts it,

> "God is at work—hidden and unremarkable as a seed itself—in Jesus and the gospel to produce a yield wholly disproportionate to human prospects and merit. The extravagant sowing that seemed mistaken and futile is vindicated by a bumper crop."
>
> (*The Gospel According to Luke,* page 237)

Two Ways to Hear

Jesus tells this parable in order to produce an effect in his hearers. He does not merely aim to inform us, as if it were enough that we understand why it is that some people reject the word while others embrace it. Instead, Jesus is alerting the crowds (and us) to the eternal significance of the way that we hear his word. Jesus concludes his parable with an ominous warning that we should hear him, if we have the spiritual ears to do so.

The disciples have received a rare gift; the "knowledge of the secrets of the kingdom of God" (**v 10**) has been given to them. Jesus was speaking the truth to them and giving them the power to comprehend it. These things are called "secrets," not because they are obscure and shadowy, but because they can only be known if God chooses to reveal them. They are God's secrets: he can choose to divulge or withhold them as he wishes, and in his kindness he has revealed these things to the disciples.

But for others, the parables may well serve as a barrier to the truth. At the end of **verse 10**, Jesus quotes from Isaiah 6:9, to the effect that there will be those who hear him (in a physical sense) but never truly hear him (in a spiritual sense). The sound of Jesus' voice reaches their ears, but the beauty and power of Jesus' message never reaches their hearts. This kind of people hear Jesus, but they don't understand him.

On the surface, this statement might seem coldhearted, as if Jesus were indifferent to the spiritual wellbeing of the "others." But in reality, the quote from Isaiah is meant to have the effect of shocking the crowd into truly hearing. As Snodgrass puts it,

"There is hope, but only if the shock of the Isaiah quotation has its **illocutionary** effect to cause hearing. The kingdom of God is a kingdom that comes through the word; it is a kingdom that is first proclaimed and then must be received and rejoiced in."

(*Stories With Intent*, page 162)

Consider Carefully

In order to help us interpret the Parable of the Sower, Luke records for us Jesus' saying about the lamp and the stand (Luke **8:16**, repeated almost word for word in 11:33). An oil lamp produced roughly as much light as a candle would, and so in order for it to be most useful, it needed to be elevated on a stand. To put such a light under a bed or in a clay jar would defeat the purpose of the lamp entirely. Here the lampstand characterizes Jesus' teaching, which serves as a lampstand to broadcast the truth of God. God has not hidden the light of the good news under a bed (**8:17**), but he has sent his Son to reveal the "secrets of the kingdom of God" (**v 10**).

The four soils are distinguished by how they hear (or respond to) this light on a stand. Some hear the word with a good heart. These are the ones who have and who "will be given more" (**v 18**); they will bear fruit exponentially and receive many blessings from Christ. Those who hear the word with a bad heart ultimately find that they have lost it. Something snatches it away or kills the word in them; even what they think they have possessed will be taken from them. Jesus mentions them at the end of **verse 18**. In light of all of this, Jesus issues a solemn warning to his hearers that they must "consider carefully how you listen."

It is clear that it is not enough to merely hear the word. It's not even enough to acknowledge the truth of Jesus' message and identity (see v 28). Instead, to truly "hear" Jesus' message means to internalize and obey it. That is the point of Jesus' reaction to the news of the arrival of his mother and brothers in **verses 19-20**. His comment that, "My mother and brothers are those who hear God's word and put it into practice" (**v 21**) should not be understood in a way that is disrespectful to his family. Instead, Jesus is taking the opportunity to make an important point: there is a kind of family that is closer than that based on a merely biological relationship. Those who not only merely hear the word but also put it into practice are truly his disciples. Jesus' "people" are not related to him by blood but by obedience to his message.

Jesus has already raised this issue in 6:46-49, where he compared someone who hears him and obeys him to someone who builds his house on a rock. And in the end, this is the crucial difference between the soils in Jesus' parable. All four soils receive the seed; they "hear" the word. But the first three do not hear it rightly. They do not embrace it and put it into practice; the seed never produces results in their actions. We are warned, says Snodgrass, to,

> "hear and respond with a lifestyle that 'bears fruit,' that is, a lifestyle marked by obedience to God as revealed in the message of Jesus." (*Stories With Intent*, page 171)

You would do well to examine your life: do you exercise care in how you respond to the word of God? Can you point to places in your life where you have done something (or refrained from doing something) simply because you wanted to put Jesus' words into practice? Are you able to discern the threats to the growth of "the seed" in your life? Are there ways that you have allowed the devil, or life's trials, or the deceitfulness of riches to choke out the growth of God's word? These are literally matters of eternal consequence; those who do not respond with this kind of belief will not be saved (**8:12**).

How you respond to the word of God is literally a matter of eternal consequence.

Questions for reflection

1. What impact should the truth that only God can reveal the "secret" of his kingdom make on: your humility? your prayers? your witness?

2. How can you see a crop of fruitfulness and godliness being grown in your own life?

3. Consider the questions in the paragraph above. Does anything need to change in how you listen to God's word?

PART TWO

Luke now transitions from the importance of listening to Jesus' teaching to focusing on Jesus' actions. The second half of Luke 8 consists of three dramatic stories covering four of Jesus' miracles. Each story emphasizes Jesus' power and authority and **implicitly** calls for a response in those who hear about it.

Power Over the Storm

"One day" (**v 22**), at Jesus' suggestion, he and the disciples set out to sail across the Sea of Galilee. After Jesus fell asleep, a violent "squall" came up and put the boat in grave danger (**v 23**). With some veteran fishermen in their midst, the disciples were well equipped to determine the degree of danger this storm presented; their panicked reaction in **verse 24** indicates that the situation was dire. They cry out to Jesus for help ("Master, Master, we're going to drown!"), and even though their panic is more than a little unseemly, he responds by calming the storm with a word. Jesus does not do anything; he doesn't put up his arms and hold the storm back. He simply tells the storm to stop and it obeys him.

Anyone who has experienced a storm at sea will be able to feel the visceral impact of this story. When Jesus speaks, the raging cacophony gives way to quiet. When Jesus rebukes the storm, the pitching and rolling of the ship gives way to calm. When Jesus is present, terror gives way to peace.

Luke's brief account ends in **verse 25** with complementary questions—questions that invite the reader to ponder them and apply them to themselves. The disciples ask, "Who is this? He commands even the winds and the water, and they obey him." The answer, they know, is that only God can control these kinds of forces:

"The LORD does whatever pleases him,
in the heavens and on the earth,
in the seas and all their depths.

He makes clouds rise from the ends of the earth;
  he sends lightning with the rain
  and brings out the wind from his storehouses."

(Psalm 135:6-7)

Jesus, for his part, wonders where the disciples' faith has gone. And so the implicit question for us is: What kind of faith do we have?

It is easy to trust God when the sailing is smooth. We enjoy God's help and blessings when we can see how everything is going to work out well. But we can tell a great deal about what we really believe about Jesus' identity when we see how we respond in a time of crisis. Do we panic and wonder if he really cares about us? Or are we able to trust him in the storms of life? We need to feel that challenge. And then we need to remember the good news—that Jesus helps the disciples (and us) even though they fail to trust him in the way that they should.

Power Over Demons

Jesus moves from a storm at sea to a storm in the life of a truly wretched man. Arriving on the eastern shore of the Sea of Galilee (a largely Gentile region), Jesus is "met by a demon-possessed man from the town" (Luke **8:27**). Luke has already mentioned that Jesus had a ministry of casting demons out of people (see 4:31-35; 6:18), but this man's condition is by far the most vivid and pathetic picture we have recorded anywhere in Scripture of what it looks like to be afflicted by a demon.

To make matters worse, this man was not simply possessed by one singular demon. Instead he was possessed by many demons (**8:30**): so many that they could call themselves "Legion" (roughly akin to the idea of "Battalion"). This man lived in the tombs outside the city, where he would roam around unclothed (**v 27**), unable to be shackled for his own benefit or the safety of others (**v 29**).

This story has an almost cinematic feel to it—something like the showdown scene in *The Good, the Bad, and the Ugly*. We can imagine Jesus stepping off the boat while "The Ecstasy of Gold" plays in the background. The calmer of the sea has come to battle the battalion of demons! But there's no battle; this is not a fair fight between equal powers.

Instead the man, at the behest of the demons, falls at Jesus' feet (**v 28**). The Greek word Luke uses there (*proskunein*) denotes bowing down before something in worship. So the demons fall down before Jesus in recognition of his authority, calling him the "Son of the Most High God." So here in a Gentile-dominated area, a platoon of demons strong enough to kill two thousand pigs bows down before Jesus and proclaims his unique identity as the Son of the only God. The posse of demons cowers before Jesus, begging repeatedly not to be sent into the realm of the dead ("the Abyss," **v 31**) and acknowledging him as the Son of the Most High (**v 28**). Jesus exhibits his power by interrogating them and giving them permission to enter a large herd of pigs, all of whom promptly rush into the lake and drown (**v 32-33**).

Some people object to Jesus' actions on ethical grounds: surely he could have performed this miracle without the loss of **porcine** life and the financial consequences that would have followed from the innocent swineherd who just lost his livelihood. Those questions are perhaps natural, but they represent a spectacular exercise in missing the point! This was the Pharisees' specialty; they could react to the healing of a blind man by complaining about making spit-mud on the Sabbath (see John 9:16). They could celebrate the healing of a cripple by raging that he had used his new-found health to carry a mat on the Sabbath (see John 5:10). There are good responses to objections about Jesus' actions in this passage (such as a discussion of the priority of human life over that of animals), but they really are not necessary. If a man conquers with a mere word a posse of demons that couldn't be restrained by chains, he doesn't need to defend his actions.

In any event, the exorcism had its effect; the man was "cured" (Luke **8:36**) and restored to his right mind (**v 35**). When Jesus went to leave, the man pleaded to go with him (**v 38**), perhaps because he wanted to learn from Jesus or because he understood that Jesus could protect him from further demonic attack. Instead of bringing the man along, however, Jesus commissions him as a witness to the power and mercy that he has received (**v 39**). The former lunatic is now a trophy to the power and grace of the Son of the Most High. He serves as an example to all of us who have experienced the mercy of Jesus; let us all declare how much Jesus has done for us!

Be Afraid, but Don't Be Afraid...

There is a fascinating **trajectory** in both of these miraculous events. At the outset we see people who are consumed by fear, first of a raging storm and then of a raging group of demons. Next, relative calm is established after Jesus exercises incredible power. But then from that calm grows a seemingly even greater fear of Jesus. Once the sea had been calmed, the disciples were gripped by "fear and amazement" (**v 25**). When the townspeople hear the eyewitness report of the swine-tenders (**v 34**), they come to see for themselves what Jesus has done (**v 35-36**). But instead of responding to Jesus' help with gratitude and worship, they ask him to leave "because they were overcome with fear" (**v 37**).

What accounts for these strange responses? We have already seen Peter's desire for Jesus to depart from him after the miraculous catch of fish (5:8), and in a similar way the disciples and the townspeople here are probably justified in feeling fear in light of these manifestations of divine power that far exceeds the greatest storm or fiercest horde of demons. The disciples' question in **8:25** ("Who is this?") is answered in **verse 28** by an unlikely source; he is the "Son of the Most High."

But their fear does seem to misunderstand the fundamental point of Jesus' presence. It may well be terrifying for sinners to be in the presence of God (e.g. Isaiah 6:5), but the Son of the Most High took on flesh not to terrify people but to save them. The arrival of God in our midst is "good news that will cause great joy" (Luke 2:10), not terror—because it is evidence that God is for us, not against us. It is evidence that he is not remote and disinterested in our suffering, as the disciples must have surely wondered when Jesus slept through the raging storm (**8:23-24**; see also Mark 4:38).

If he were our enemy, God would be terrifying, and unmitigated fear would most certainly be called for; the demons are correct to be afraid. But since God is "for us" in Christ, his power is actually a wonderful antidote to fear. What exactly do we have to worry about if Jesus, the powerful Son of the Most High, is on our side? If Jesus can calm a raging storm and conquer a host of demons, what problems in your life are beyond his power to help you? If you are overcome with fear, perhaps Jesus would ask you the same question that he asked his disciples: "Where is your faith?" (Luke **8:25**).

Power For the Desperate

In the final section of chapter 8, Luke pulls out the stories of two very different individuals that Jesus met upon his return to the Galilean side of the lake (**v 40**). The first individual was a man named Jairus, a "synagogue leader" (**v 41**). That was a formal position in the life of the synagogue, and it carried with it a host of practical responsibilities for the spiritual life of the community. As such, Jairus was undoubtedly an important and respected member of society.

The woman that we meet in **verse 43** has a drastically different station in life; she is an unnamed woman whose condition was beyond all hope. She was "subject to bleeding for twelve years," a **euphemism** for some sort of **gynaecological** malady that "no one could heal." To make matters worse, the woman's condition would have meant that she was an outcast from society. Because of her bleeding, she was ceremonially unclean (see Leviticus 15:25) and would pass her uncleanness on to anyone who touched her. If she was a young woman, then this condition may very well have prevented her from having children—a particularly isolating condition in that society.

In short, you would be hard pressed to find two more different people in that town than Jairus and this unnamed woman. But they have one very important thing in common: they are both suffering terribly. They are both at the end of their rope with no other options; they need Jesus' help badly. For Jairus, despite all of his respectability, has a desperate problem: his twelve-year-old daughter is dying (Luke **8:42**). He throws himself at Jesus' feet and pleads for his assistance (**v 41**). And so these two very different people find themselves at the same place at the same time, both wanting Jesus' help.

As Jesus was on his way to help Jairus, the woman approached him to touch his cloak. It is not clear why she thought that touching Jesus would heal her, but surprisingly enough it was effective: immediately her bleeding stopped (**v 44**). In just a moment, twelve years of frustration and futility are reversed.

Jesus did not see the woman who touched him in the pressing crowd, but he did notice that power had gone out of him (**v 45-46**). The symbolism in the meeting is remarkable: blood flows from the sick woman, but the power to heal flows from Jesus. Her touch was supposed to transmit uncleanness, but instead Jesus' touch transformed her and made her clean.

> Jesus is not content just to dispatch a miracle, for he wants an encounter with a person.

It seems that this woman wanted nothing to do with an actual encounter with Jesus, for at first she did not admit what she had done (**v 45**). She may have hoped to sneak in without creating a fuss, get her healing, and get out without anyone realizing what had happened. But Jesus won't let her slip away quietly. He is not content just to dispatch a miracle, for he wants an encounter with a person. And so finally, "seeing that she could not go unnoticed," she came trembling to Jesus to tell him the truth (**v 47**). Imagine how her heart must have leapt after Jesus started talking, and the first word out of his mouth was a gentle one: "Daughter"!

Jesus was looking for her so that he could correct her misunderstanding of what had happened. She might have thought that she was healed by touching Jesus' cloak, as if by magic. But Jesus wants her to know that it was actually her faith that healed her (**v 48**; see 7:50).

The joyous scene is brought to a screeching halt, however, by a messenger from Jairus' house bringing crushing news that his daughter has died (**8:49**). It seems that Jesus' kindness toward the sick woman may have cost this little girl her only chance of living. But Jesus is undeterred by the report, and he proceeds to Jairus' house anyway, taking a few disciples and the girl's parents inside with him (**v 51**). His command to the mourners in the home ("Stop wailing") and his assertion that she was merely asleep (**v 52**) would have seemed ludicrous; surely they knew a dead body when they saw one (**v 53**). (In reality, of course, they were right; the girl's spirit had departed from her body, **v 55**. We should understand Jesus' comment about her being asleep to mean that she would soon wake up.)

Just as in the creation account (Genesis 1:1-31) God's word has power to bring life into being, so Jesus' command imparts life to the young girl (Luke **8:54**). His instruction to give her something to eat (**v 55**) signifies a return to a completely functioning life. Understandably, "her parents were astonished" (**v 56**) and Jesus ordered them not to tell anyone (see 4:41), most likely to prevent the crowds from getting wrong-headed ideas about him coming to establish a political kingdom.

Luke's account of these two miracles leaves us breathless. In the span of a few short verses we are taken on a roller-coaster ride from sorrow to joy to despair back to joy. And these events make for a perfect conclusion to the chapter, for yet again we see the issue of fear come to the surface. Like the disciples in the boat, both sufferers are understandably fearful in the storms of their lives: the sick woman trembles in Jesus' presence (**8:47**) and Jairus is afraid that his daughter is lost forever (**v 50**). But yet again Jesus' bearing and actions invite us to come to him in faith when we are consumed with suffering or fear; he is powerful and he is kind. He has come to bring an end to our fear; he is powerful enough to do it and he welcomes us to come to him in our time of need.

Questions for reflection

1. How have the pictures of Jesus that Luke gives us here thrilled you, and moved you to worship him?

2. "Don't be afraid; just believe." Is there any way in which you need to let these words comfort and calm you right now?

3. Are there any Christians you know who are walking through a storm, and with whom you could share an encouragement drawn from this passage?

8. SATISFACTION, SHOCKS, AND SELF-DENIAL

Up until this point, Jesus' mission has largely been a solitary one. With the exception of some complementary preaching from John, Jesus has been the only person preaching the good news of the kingdom (4:43; 8:1) and performing powerful signs of the kingdom's arrival (7:21; 8:22-56). But now a change is ushered in as Jesus summons "the Twelve" (**9:1**) and sends them out (**v 2**) with a two-fold mission that mirrors Jesus' own actions up to this point: "to proclaim the kingdom of God and to heal the sick" (**v 2, 6**). The one-man show just became a group enterprise.

Come, So You May Go

The order here is important; the disciples are first summoned to Jesus and only then are they sent out. Nothing that we have seen so far would make us think that the disciples are prepared or qualified for such a mission, but Jesus "gave them power and authority" that they would need in order "to drive out all demons and to cure diseases" (**v 1**). Thankfully for them (and for us), the power for mission comes not from something within the ones who are sent out, but from the Lord himself (see 24:47-49).

Jesus' instructions for the Twelve begin with what they should not bring with them: "No staff, no bag, no bread, no money, no extra shirt" (**9:3**). In short, Jesus denies them all of the things that someone would normally depend upon on a long journey. As the disciples go, they will be continually aware of their need and dependence; their mission will require them to act on their faith in Jesus. Surely their debrief with Jesus upon their return (**v 10**) contained many examples of the Lord's provision for all of their needs.

There are also specific ways that Jesus would have the disciples interact with the people they meet along the way. Once they get to a town, they should be gracious guests, staying in one house if possible (**v 4**) rather than looking for an upgrade in their accommodations. If they do not receive a welcome in a certain location, they should treat that town as if it were an unclean **heathen** village, shaking the dust of that town off their feet (**v 5**), lest it follow them and pollute the next place to which they go. Failure to respond to the proclamation of the good news has dire consequences.

The Confusion of a King

Luke has already warned his readers that John has been imprisoned by Herod Antipas (3:19-20); now we discover through the tetrarch's private musings that John has been beheaded (**9:9**). But when Herod became aware of "all that was going on" (**v 7**), he was "perplexed" by the opinions about Jesus that were being bandied about. The three lines of speculations—that Jesus might be John returned from the dead or Elijah or another prophet of old (**v 7-8**)—are reflected in Peter's response to Jesus' question about who the crowds say that he is (**v 18-19**).

Herod's question about Jesus boils down to one that is familiar to us by now: *Who is this?* (**v 9**—see 8:25). In order to answer that question, Herod "tried to see him," a wish that would be fulfilled in the final scenes of Jesus' earthly life (23:8-11). At that time, it would become clear that Herod's interest in Jesus is limited to seeing a sign from him, a desire that Jesus would not indulge and that would result in Herod treating Jesus with contempt. Speculation about Jesus has reached even as far as the palace, but even the ruler of the land lacks clarity about who he really is. By including this brief digression, Luke prepares us to appreciate Peter's startlingly clear confession of Jesus as the Christ in the coming section (**9:20**).

Feeding the Five Thousand

With his disciples having returned to Jesus from their stint as itinerant preachers, they all "withdrew by themselves to a town called Bethsaida" (**v 10**) just to the north of the Sea of Galilee. They were not by themselves for long, however, because the crowds discovered their plans and followed them. Far from being exasperated by the crowds, Jesus "welcomed them" and, following the pattern we have come to expect from his ministry, he taught them and healed those in need of help (**v 11**).

The presence of so many people means that Jesus' little band of disciples have no hope of being by themselves, but it turns out that there is a far more pressing concern. As the day goes on, a potential crisis is brewing: there is no way to provide food for a crowd this size in such a "remote place" (**v 12**). The Twelve suggest that Jesus should dismiss the crowd into the surrounding area to find food and a place to stay—a perfectly logical suggestion on the face of it. Jesus' solution, "You [**emphatic**] give them something to eat" (**v 13**), seems much less reasonable in the face of the scarcity of resources. Five loaves and two fish would not make a dent in the hunger of five thousand men (**v 14**—compare this to 2 Kings 4:42-44), and the cost of buying food for that many people would be prohibitive. (The Greek word in Luke **9:14** has the sense of "males"—there may well have been women and children present in addition). Yet again Jesus has brought his disciples into a situation where the needs of the moment far outstrip their resources and abilities (see 8:23). And just as in previous situations, Jesus uses the difficult circumstances to display his divine power and instruct his disciples.

If you think about it, Jesus surely could have fed the crowd by himself. But in his kindness he involved the disciples in the work, and as a result they got the joy of service and a lesson about Jesus' power.

In the same way Jesus still involves his people in the work of ministry, giving us more resources than we need so that we can have the joy of caring for others.

And just as the disciples could only go out to preach and cure diseases and cast out demons because Jesus gave them power and authority (**9:1**), so they could only obey his command to feed the crowd (**v 13**) if Jesus himself miraculously provided the bread. In **verse 16**, that is exactly what happens, as Jesus gives thanks for the bread and then gives it to the disciples to distribute among the people. They minister to the people but only because Jesus has given them everything they need to do so. That pattern holds true for the disciples of Jesus today; we have nothing to give away to others unless Christ has given us the power and resources that we need.

> We have nothing to give away to others unless Christ gives us the power and resources we need.

As we piece together our understanding of who Jesus is, the miraculous feeding of the 5,000 men is an important clue. Edwards notes three places in Luke's Gospel where we are told that Jesus takes bread, thanks God for it, breaks it, and then gives it to people. The first of these is found in this passage (**v 16**), the second occurs at the Last Supper (22:19), and the third takes place at the meal at Emmaus (24:30). Each of these is a point in Luke's narrative where there is a profound recognition of Jesus' identity and mission. As he explains,

> "Luke thus employs the formula 'took/blessed/broke/gave' in three critical and calculated contexts, in each instance of which the breaking and dispensing of bread to the disciples is a revelatory symbol of Jesus' self-giving for the church in his passion and resurrection, through which his disciples recognize him (24:31) as the fulfillment of Scripture (24:32)."

(The Gospel According to Luke, page 266)

Satisfied

Luke's account of this miracle is rich with Old Testament echoes. The command to split the crowd up into groups of "fifty each" (**9:14-15**) is reminiscent of the ministries of Moses (see Exodus 18:21 and Deuteronomy 1:15) and of Elijah (1 Kings 18:13). The provision of bread in a remote place is reminiscent of the Lord's gift of manna in the Israelites' flight from Egypt (Exodus 16:14-15)—a story that will be brought to the front in the upcoming transfiguration narrative (Luke 9:28-36). The "twelve basketfuls" that were gathered up (**v 17**) remind us of the twelve tribes of Israel.

The point is that Jesus is the one who is able to provide richly for Israel. Isaiah had seen a coming day when the Lord would provide for his people "a feast of rich food for all peoples, a banquet of aged wine—the best of meats and the finest of wines" (Isaiah 25:6). When Jesus provides a feast for his people, it is abundant. Luke stresses that everyone who was there ate and was satisfied. And even after everyone ate as much as they wanted, there was plenty left over; Jesus' resources were not close to being exhausted.

Eating food is a universal and intimate experience. It is no wonder that food and feasting and eating are so frequently used as spiritual metaphors in Scripture. Spiritual blessings are sometimes described in terms of physical food (see Isaiah 55:1-3; Luke 14:5-24 and John 6:27). Mary understood that God is the one who "has filled the hungry with good things" (Luke 1:53), and here we see the truth of this enacted.

Jesus calls himself the bread of life (John 6:35), and even demands that we feast on him if we would be his disciples. When we see Jesus providing bread for the masses, we should be alerted to the fact that there is a deeper truth being illustrated.

Even in places where food is abundant, there is a spiritual hunger that abounds in every human heart. Our souls all long for the peace and meaning and purpose that can only come from knowing God and being known by him. In the absence of those things, people will look in any number of places to find deep soul-satisfaction: success, money, entertainment, relationships, sex, family, even religious perfor- mance. All of those things can be very good in their proper context, but none of them can bear the weight of our soul's longing. None of them can satisfy the hunger of our hearts. Like a thirsty man drinking seawater, the more we consume of these things to quench our soul's longing, the worse the problem becomes. The problem is not primarily with our desire for satisfaction, but rather, where we look for it. It is an expression of our fallen nature that we look for fulfillment in such unsatisfying places.

The great news is that Jesus can feed our starving souls until they can't eat any more. He has promised that those who hunger will be satisfied (Luke 6:21). In that remote place, everyone was hungry. And there, with no other means of provision, every single person who looked to Jesus for help was able to eat until he was fully satisfied. That is the hope for us, that we can come to Jesus with our seemingly insurmountable need and find that he can satisfy us completely.

Can you feel the hunger of your soul? Hear God's invitation to you to come to Jesus and eat your fill.

Questions for reflection

1. When it comes to proclaiming and showing the kingdom, do you need to rely on Jesus for what you are doing... or do you need to remember that Jesus gives you what you need, so that you start doing?

2. Where do you tend to look for satisfaction, other than to Jesus? Have you found that fulfilling, or disappointing?

3. What would it mean for you to "come to Jesus and eat your fill"?

PART TWO

It is an indication of how extraordinary a thing it was to be in the presence of Jesus that the question of his true identity has been woven like a thread through Luke's narrative. It is not often that the words and deeds of an individual cause their contemporaries to struggle with the nature of that person's existence. But we have seen the question, "Who is this?" asked repeatedly by different people in different places (4:22; 5:21; 7:19; 7:49; 8:25; 9:9). And while we have seen the correct answer to that question in the mouths of angels (2:11) and demons (4:34; 8:28), up to this point we are still waiting for Jesus' disciples to put all of the pieces together and come up with the truth.

A Confession

It is in that context that Jesus was praying alone one day (**9:18**). Perhaps he was praying that his disciples would have clarity about who he was, for when they came along he put the question to them, "Who do the crowds say I am?" The disciples reply in **verse 19** with the same three options that had so perplexed Herod in verses 7-8: John the Baptist, Elijah, or some prophet of old. All three of those options would have been seen as positive opinions; clearly popular opinion regarding Jesus was favorable. But Jesus is not concerned primarily with public opinion; he wants to have a personal conversation with his disciples. So in **verse 20** he presses them for their personal conviction.

Peter, presumably speaking on behalf of the others, replies: "God's Messiah." "Messiah" is a Hebrew word that simply means "anointed." In the Old Testament kings were anointed for the tasks to which they were called, and God had promised that he would one day send an heir of David who would sit on this throne and rule in a greater kingdom than his ancestor had known (2 Samuel 7:12-13; Psalm 2; Jeremiah 23:5; Luke 1:32-33). The title "Messiah" was "consistently used to refer to the expected royal Davidic figure" (Carson and Beale,

Commentary on the New Testament Use of the Old Testament, page 311). Peter's declaration that Jesus is the Messiah is bold and clear. He is saying that Jesus was that long-awaited anointed ruler.

What is far more breathtaking, though, is Jesus' response; he actually embraces what Peter says! In Matthew's account of these events, Jesus explicitly affirms Peter's confession in the strongest terms (Matthew 16:17). That in and of itself does not make Jesus unique; history is full of **megalomaniacal cult** leaders who had delusions along these lines. But they all eventually faded from the scene because the truth was obvious to all but their small band of hoodwinked followers.

But among the religious leaders who have actually established a following among reasonable people, only Jesus thought that he was the Messiah sent by God to save the world. Near the beginning of his chapter on Buddhism in *The Religions of Man*, Huston Smith, who specializes in world religions and is not a follower of Jesus in any traditional sense, writes:

"How many people have provoked this question: not 'Who are you?' with respect to name, origin, or ancestry, but 'What are you?'—what order of being do you belong to, what species do you represent? Not Caesar, certainly. Not Napoleon, not even Socrates. Only two, Jesus and Buddha. When the people carried their puzzlement to the Buddha himself, the answer he gave provided a handle for his entire message. 'Are you a god?' they asked. 'No.' 'An angel?' 'No.' 'A saint?' 'No.' 'Then what are you?' Buddha answered, 'I am awake.'" (page 80)

Buddha **demurred**, but Jesus was not shy about acknowledging who he was. Buddha insisted that he was not the point, but Jesus affirms Peter's confession. Jesus is unique on the world stage: someone who thought of himself in the highest terms and yet was a compelling and attractive presence. Out of all the religious thinkers in human history, none makes a claim (or, in this case, allows a claim to be made about himself) like Jesus.

A Shocking Plan

We might expect that the follow-up to Peter's declaration would be a triumphant celebration and a worldwide broadcast of the big news. Instead, Jesus "strictly warned" them not to tell anyone this truth (Luke **9:21**). This prohibition is temporary—once Jesus has been raised from the dead, the disciples will be empowered and expected to take the message about Jesus into the world (see Acts 1:8)—but it is surprising.

We are not told exactly why Jesus sets down this prohibition, but the next thing that Jesus says makes it seem that he doesn't want this word to get around because he doesn't want there to be confusion about what kind of Messiah he's going to be. The expectation was that the Messiah would come from God as a mighty military commander—a warrior who would throw off the oppressors of God's people and take over as God's King on the throne (see John 6:15). Of course, there is an element of truth in that belief. Bock points out that Jesus will eventually exercise authority over the whole world. But not at this moment:

> "The misunderstanding that is so dangerous is one of timing, not substance." (*Luke 1:1–9:50*, page 846, note 4)

Jesus makes it abundantly clear in the next verses that his messianic ministry would not begin with political triumph and military conquest.

Instead, "The Son of Man must suffer many things and be rejected by the elders, the chief priests and the teachers of the law, and he must be killed" (Luke **9:22**). Jesus is God's Messiah, but the path that he will travel is not one of quick glory, but of terrible suffering. The paradoxes are stark; Jesus is talking about the Messiah and the Son of Man (both titles that **connote** glory and power) in terms of the Suffering Servant of Isaiah (see Isaiah 52:13 – 53:12). The most glorious One will suffer greatly and then be rejected and killed, not by the enemies of Israel but by its leadership. He will show his power by allowing others to have power over him. When he is at the mercy

> There is an incredible love that stands behind Jesus' statement that the Son of Man "must" suffer.

of others, he is simply doing what he knows "must" happen according to his Father's decree.

There is an incredible love that stands behind Jesus' statement that the Son of Man "must" suffer. Nothing outside of God constrains him or forces him to do anything that he does not wish to do, but the necessity of the Christ's suffering is rooted in God's free decision to take away the sins of his people and restore them to himself. These things "must" happen only because God loved the world so much that he sent his Son to die for sinners.

A Shocking Call

There is yet another "must" before Jesus' teaching is complete. The Son of Man must suffer, and in light of that suffering an obligation is placed on anyone who wants to be his disciple. A disciple of Jesus "must deny themselves and take up their cross daily and follow" him (Luke **9:23**). It is important to notice the scope of what Jesus is saying; "whoever" would be a follower of Jesus "must" comply with these directions. They are not reserved for a special class of super-disciples and **martyrs**, and they are not optional.

All of Jesus' followers must "deny themselves." We might think of self-denial in terms of refraining from luxuries, as when a person on a budget must deny herself some frivolous purchase or a person on a diet decides to deny himself dessert. But Jesus is calling his people to something much more radical.

John Stott comments on this passage:

"To deny ourselves is to behave towards ourselves as Peter did towards Jesus when he denied him three times. The verb is the same (*aparneomai*). He disowned him, repudiated him, turned his back on him. Self-denial is not denying to ourselves luxuries such as chocolates, cakes, cigarettes and cocktails (although it might include this); it is actually denying or disowning ourselves, renouncing our supposed right to go our own way. To deny oneself is to turn from the **idolatry** of self-centeredness. "

(*The Cross of Christ*, page 272)

That being the case, we can understand why all followers of Jesus must deny themselves. Any attempt at discipleship that does not involve renouncing **autonomy** and self-love is not actually following Jesus in any meaningful way. If we would make him our master, we must first remove ourselves from that position.

Perhaps our modern familiarity with the cross as a piece of jewelry or a decoration in a church building has robbed Jesus' next statement of much of its scandal. In Jesus' day, a cross was a disgusting thing, akin perhaps to a lynch mob's noose in its capacity to create a **visceral** dread in those who saw it. It was a cruel method of execution, used by the Romans to keep people in the provinces from rebelling.

When Jesus says that anyone who wants to be a disciple of his must pick up their cross (**v 23**), he is speaking in the starkest of terms. Romans required the condemned to carry the horizontal piece of their cross to the execution site; a man who was carrying his cross was on a one-way trip to death. Jesus is not talking about physical death, though it's possible that following Jesus in this radical way could cost you your life. Instead, Jesus is talking about dying to your old way of life and crucifying the old, self-centered way of living. Following Jesus is like a kind of death because every area of a disciple's life is radically changed: our

> If we would make Christ our master, we must first remove ourselves from that position.

finances, ambitions, sexuality, entertainments, and relationships must all be brought into conformity with the wishes of Jesus. As a follower of Jesus makes the daily choice to pick up his cross, every part of that day will be impacted.

Jesus frames his call of discipleship in extreme terms, using words like "whoever" and "must," and in so doing he excludes anyone who wants some other kind of discipleship. It is a daily activity—not merely a decision made once and left to the wayside. Picking up one's cross is the most extreme way to describe the self-denial required of disciples. If we take Jesus' words seriously, we have to admit that much that passes for Christianity today will eventually be revealed as a **diabolic counterfeit**.

Positive feelings about Jesus, a commitment to social justice, a general posture of moral uprightness… none of these things are proof that we belong to Jesus. The only kind of Christ-following is self-denying, cross-bearing discipleship. It is important to remember, however, that we are not saved by taking up our cross. Rather, we are saved because Jesus took up his cross for us. He does not call his followers to anything that he has not done for us first.

A Strange Sales Pitch

It seems that Jesus would make a terrible salesman. In these verses he violates every principle of effective evangelism and every popular church-growth strategy. Any marketer would tell Jesus that if you want people to follow you, you should emphasize the benefits of discipleship and try to draw attention away from whatever attendant costs there might be. But here he leads with the cost of discipleship!

But in God's economy, losing one's life is actually the path to blessing. If someone wants to "save" his life by refusing to pick up the cross of discipleship and by clinging desperately to his rights and privileges, he will find in the end that he has lost it (**v 24**). Whatever he has gained in the process of clinging tightly to his life will be lost in the end; even if he gains the entire world along the way, what good will that do him (**v 25**)? Paradoxically, the call to pick up your cross is a call to come and save your life.

When a condemned man carried his cross, it was a public spectacle. In the same way, following Jesus is a public event. If a would-be disciple is ashamed of him and his words and will not confess him publicly, Jesus himself will be ashamed of him when he returns in judgment (**v 26**—see 12:8 for the same principle stated positively). If we deny our relationship to Jesus before men, he will deny that we are his on the last day. When that happens, the one who has sought to retain his life by refusing the cross of discipleship will find that he has forfeited his "very self" (**9:25**).

In the days when Luke was writing, Christians were being persecuted, imprisoned, and even killed for their faith in Jesus. For first-century Christians (as well as believers in many contexts around the world today), the temptation to be ashamed of Jesus was sometimes a temptation to self-preservation. As Western societies become more hostile to Jesus' claim to be the truth and the only way to God, believers in those contexts will have to decide whether they are willing to be insulted and thought less of (or even worse) for their connection to Jesus.

Jesus' words are sobering. The arrival of God's Messiah has set in motion a chain of events that will lead inevitably to his suffering and ultimate return "in his glory and in the glory of the Father and of the holy angels" (**v 26**). The clock is ticking; Jesus even promised that "some who are standing here will not taste death before they see the kingdom of God" (**v 27**). The exact meaning of Jesus' words here is debated; Bock summarizes the four views helpfully (in *Luke 1:1–9:50*, pages 858-859):

1. Jesus (mistakenly, as it turns out) believed that the full and consummated kingdom is coming in the very near future. This makes Jesus a misguided prophet of the apocalypse.

2. Jesus is referring to the reality of the kingdom as it is inaugurated either in his resurrection and ascension or at the coming of the Holy Spirit at Pentecost.

> It is madness to continue living as if this present world were the ultimate reality.

3. Jesus is talking about the transfiguration (see v 28-36), which is a display of his glorious kingdom and a promise that Jesus will one day come in his full glory.

4. Jesus is prophesying the destruction of Jerusalem (in AD 70), which served as a foretaste of God's judgment.

Clearly, given all we have seen of and heard from Jesus so far, the first possibility is to be rejected. In context, I think Jesus seems to be referring to his vindication at his resurrection and ascension into heaven (see 22:69)—the second option above. But whether Jesus means options 2, 3 or 4, his point is nonetheless clear: in light of the imminent arrival of his kingdom, it is madness to continue living as if this present world were the ultimate reality.

If a disciple must pick up her cross daily, then perhaps we should see embedded in that reality a call to daily self-examination:

- What am I living for?

- What am I hoping to gain by my actions today?

- How long will those things last?

- What would it mean to lose my life today in order to save it in the end?

Given the challenging nature of Christ's words to his followers here, we should expect our answers to those questions never to be anything less than deeply challenging.

Questions for reflection

1. What did you find most challenging in these verses?

2. How can a Christian carry their cross and yet also be joyful?

3. Spend some time answering the questions in the final paragraph.

9. AT THE PEAK AND IN THE VALLEY

At the outset of his public ministry, Jesus received a divine endorsement in the form of a voice from heaven saying, "You are my Son, whom I love; with you I am well pleased" (3:22). Now Jesus, who has just revealed that as God's Messiah he will suffer and die (9:22), is about to turn his face to Jerusalem (**v 51**) to inaugurate the events that will lead to his crucifixion. At this second crucial turning point, we receive yet another confirmation of Jesus' ministry in the form of a voice from heaven.

Up the Mountain

Luke tells us that these events took place "about eight days" later (**v 28**). Eight is not a number traditionally associated with a specific meaning in Jewish literature (as opposed to seven or twelve), but it does recur in one form or another throughout Luke's Gospel. Here it may be intended to remind the reader of the period of time that elapsed between the birth of a son and his **circumcision**, a fact that Luke has already placed before his reader (1:59; 2:21). In the same way that circumcision was a response to a son's birth eight days after the fact, so these events on the mountaintop are connected to the revelation of Jesus as God's Messiah that occurred eight days earlier.

When Luke makes a point to mention that Jesus was praying, it is usually a signal that something important is about to happen (e.g. 3:21; 9:18). And so it comes as no surprise that when Jesus took his inner circle of disciples (Peter, John, and James) up an unidentified mountain, it was for the purpose of prayer (**v 28**). While he was praying and the three disciples were fighting drowsiness (**v 32**), "the appearance of his face changed, and his clothes became as bright as a flash of lightning" (**v 29**).

Once Jesus' appearance is changed, Moses and Elijah appear "in glorious splendor" and have an audience with Jesus. The importance of these two particular men is much debated, but at the very least it seems certain that they are intended to represent a witness to and continuity with the ministry of Jesus. As the symbols of the Old Testament law (Moses) and the prophetic hope of the last days (Elijah), the pair testifies to Jesus' status as the pinnacle of God's revelation and plan.

A New Exodus

This account of the transfiguration is the only one to give us a glimpse into the conversation between these three dazzling figures. "They spoke about his departure, which he was about to bring to fulfillment at Jerusalem" (**v 31**). Here Luke chooses an unusual word to indicate the subject of this extraordinary conversation. Literally, the word that Luke uses to indicate Jesus' death and resurrection is "exodus." The event that "he was about to bring to fulfillment in Jerusalem" is referred to as "his exodus."

That is significant because the exodus from Egypt was the foundational event in the formation of the nation of Israel. It was the **paradigm** of salvation in the Old Testament; when the people of Israel needed to be reminded of how the Lord had redeemed them, the example of the exodus was always close at hand (e.g. Deuteronomy 6:12; Psalm 136:10-16). And now, Moses and Elijah are talking with Jesus about the exodus, the defining moment in God's plan of redemption. But it's not the old exodus that they are discussing; they are talking about the new one that Jesus is about to accomplish.

In the first exodus, God's people were hopelessly enslaved to a cruel tyrant. When they could not help themselves, God sent them a deliverer who led them out of bondage. And now, Jesus has come to lead his people out from an even greater slavery: slavery to sin and death (see John 8:34). Through his death and resurrection and ascension, the greater Moses will lead God's people in a greater exodus to free them from a greater bondage. Just as the first exodus created the nation of Israel, Jesus' death and resurrection and ascension essentially form the New Testament church. Just as Israelites would look back on the exodus from Egypt to remember God's love and deliverance, now Christians look back to the death and resurrection of Christ frequently in order to be reminded of the salvation that we have received.

> It is hard to imagine that the transfigured Jesus on the mountain is the same as the disfigured Jesus on the cross.

It is hard to imagine that the Jesus that we see here is the same Jesus that suffered and died for us—that the transfigured Jesus on the mountain is the same as the disfigured Jesus on the cross. Here on the Mount of Transfiguration, Jesus' clothes are bright like a flash of lightning (Luke **9:29**); at the crucifixion Jesus' clothes would be soaked in blood and divided among wicked men (23:34). On this mountain, Jesus is surrounded by Moses and Elijah in splendor (**9:30**); there he would hang between two criminals (23:33). Here he is enveloped in the cloud of God's presence (**9:34**); there he would hang on the cross in utter darkness (23:44). Here he hears the voice of his Father expressing his delight in him (**9:35**); there Jesus would be forsaken by the Father for us (Matthew 27:46).

The transfiguration puts the glory of Jesus on display in a way that is obvious to those looking on. But at the cross, the humility and love of Jesus shines through in a way that is perhaps harder to perceive at first, but ultimately is even more breathtaking. John Calvin put it this way:

> "For in the cross of Christ, as in a splendid theater, the incomparable goodness of God is set before the whole world. The glory

of God shines, indeed, in all creatures on high and below, but never more brightly than in the cross … If it be objected that nothing could be less glorious than Christ's death … I reply that in that death we see a boundless glory which is concealed from the ungodly." (Quoted in Stott, *The Cross of Christ*, page 202)

A New Tent

At first, Peter's desire to erect three shelters for Jesus, Moses, and Elijah (Luke **9:33**) seems strange. Luke tells us that Peter "did not know what he was saying," a comment that has led many to assume that the suggestion was a ludicrous one. But that's not necessarily the case. As Edwards notes,

"Luke does not say Peter 'did not know what to say,' but he 'did not know what he was saying.'"

(*The Gospel According to Luke,* page 283)

That is to say, there was more truth to what Peter was saying than even he understood.

In order to understand what is happening here, the reader needs to be familiar with an event that is recorded in Exodus 40:34-35. In those verses, Moses has just finished assembling the tabernacle, an elaborately constructed tent where God would meet with his people during their time in the wilderness. We read that after Moses finished the work, "Then the cloud covered the tent of meeting, and the glory of the LORD filled the tabernacle. Moses could not enter the tent of meeting because the cloud had settled on it, and the glory of the LORD filled the tabernacle."

Luke's account of the transfiguration makes contact with that passage in three places. First, Peter's suggestion that he might build "shelters" for Jesus, Moses, and Elijah (Luke **9:33**) uses the same Greek word (*skene*) that appears in the account of the tabernacle in Exodus 40 in the Septuagint, the Greek Old Testament. The second aspect of this passage that connects to Exodus 40 is the presence of glory. In

Moses' day, the tabernacle was filled with the shining glory of the Lord (compare Luke 2:9). On the mountain, Jesus' clothing becomes like lightning while Moses and Elijah appear "in glorious splendor" (**9:30**). Finally, just as a cloud appeared to fill the tabernacle, so the disciples on the mountain were enveloped in a terrifying cloud (**v 34**).

Far from being a mere coincidence, the thematic overlap between Luke's account and the Exodus 40 narrative points us to an important meaning in these events: Jesus is the new and better tabernacle. He is the place where the glory and presence of God dwells with his people. At the Mount of Transfiguration, the disciples saw with their own eyes what John described at the beginning of his Gospel account, "The Word became flesh and made his dwelling [the Greek word is *skenoun*, or "tabernacled"] among us. We have seen his glory, the glory of the one and only Son, who came from the Father, full of grace and truth" (John 1:14).

A Not-so-New Command

After the cloud appeared and covered them, the disciples heard a voice saying, "This is my Son, whom I have chosen; listen to him" (Luke **9:35**; see Peter's own recollection of this event in 2 Peter 1:17-18). We have already seen the importance of Jesus' status as the Son of God in Luke's Gospel (particularly in Luke 3:22 – 4:13). Here at the transfiguration, as at his baptism, Jesus' unique status as God's Son and chosen Servant is proclaimed.

Moses was one of the greatest figures in all the history of the Old Testament. He was the **mediator** who brought the Law of God to his people. He led them out of slavery in Egypt. Elijah was one of the greatest prophets in the history of Israel. But the Father looks on Jesus and says, *That's my Son!* Not Moses, not Elijah, but Jesus. Moses and Elijah were faithful servants, but Jesus is the very Son of God.

The proclamation of Jesus' status as the Son and chosen one has a practical application for us. The voice from heaven tells the three disciples what to do: "listen to him" (**9:35**). You can imagine how it would impact faithful Jews like Peter, James and John for God to look at Moses and Elijah and Jesus and say of Jesus alone, "Listen to *him*!"

Jesus, the chosen Son, is the supreme revelation of his heavenly Father. As a result, we should listen to him. This is the argument that the author of Hebrews makes at the outset of his letter: "In the past God spoke to our ancestors through the prophets at many times and in various ways, but in these last days he has spoken to us by his Son, whom he appointed heir of all things, and through whom also he made the universe" (Hebrews 1:1-2). God does not speak through Jesus in the same manner in which he spoke through prophets like Moses and Elijah. Jesus is the tabernacle, the presence of God here on earth. He *is* the **medium** of communication; he is the revelation of God. We can and should have great confidence that everything that God wants to say to us is wrapped up in the person of Jesus.

In a complicated and confusing world, this is very good news. All around us advisors abound and **mutually exclusive** opinions are offered with the utmost certainty. The world offers us a never-ending selection of things to value and treasure and listen to. How then do we decide what is right and wrong, true and false, good and evil?

Here God the Father gives us very clear guidance: listen to Jesus! Yes, Jesus' words about the nature of his kingdom can be unsettling. He went to the cross and he calls his followers to pick up their crosses as well (Luke 9:23). But we need to resist the urge to soft-pedal these statements or ignore them. We need to listen and we need to listen to him. Don't trust Oprah or Buddha or the latest guru peddling a book. Don't even listen to your own feelings and impulses. Instead, listen to Jesus, God's pleasing and chosen Son.

Questions for reflection

1. How do these verses move you to worship Jesus?

2. Is there any way that you have been resisting the call to "listen to him"? Why have you been resisting? How does this glimpse of Jesus' powerful glory motivate you toward obedience?

3. Why is it liberating, and not oppressive, to listen to and obey the King?

PART TWO

Big Comedown

The transition from the preceding verses into the next episode could hardly be more jarring. Up on the mountain Peter, James, and John had seen Jesus in unspeakable glory. But as they descend the next morning (**v 37**), they are met by a startling reminder that the world is oftentimes an ugly, broken place. On the mountaintop, they witnessed God the Father's delight in his glorious Son. In the crowd below, there is a father in agony because his only son is afflicted terribly by a demon (**v 38-39**). It is a powerful reminder that the Son of God did not come to live in glory here on earth, but to wade into human misery and set captives free (see 4:18).

Two things make this story particularly memorable. First, the child's affliction is truly pitiable. The demon's oppression of the child is described in heart-wrenching terms; the boy shrieks and is thrown into convulsions, foaming at the mouth with hardly any relief (**9:39**). It seems that the child is suffering both from a terrible physical ailment (Matthew 17:15 identifies it as epilepsy) and also from demonic oppression (note that the New Testament views these as two entirely separate conditions—e.g. Matthew 4:24). The father, like the other helpless parents in Luke's Gospel (see Luke 7:12; 8:41-42), sees his son being destroyed and can do nothing to stop it.

The other memorable feature of this incident is the disciples' inability to cast this demon out (**9:40**). Presumably the disciples in question here are the nine who did not go up on the mountain, but their inability is surprising since Jesus had previously given "authority to drive out all demons" to the entire Twelve (**v 1**). Their failure was not due to a lack of power or authority; there had to be something else at work in this situation.

Jesus' response to the father's plea is not what we might expect. In the face of terrible demonic oppression, he expresses exasperation not with the forces of evil at work in this child's suffering, but with the people around him. He indicates that there is a serious spiritual problem at work in the crowd, calling them "an unbelieving and perverse generation" (**v 41**). Those words echo the Old Testament's condemnation of Israel (e.g. Isaiah 65:2), as does Jesus' musing about how long he will have to put up with them (e.g. Numbers 14:11).

It is not clear whether it is the disciples or the larger crowd that is being addressed by Jesus' words here. Initially it seems like the latter, for it would be a strange choice of words if Jesus were referring here to just twelve people as an entire "generation." But Mark records for us a conversation that takes place at the end of this incident where the disciples ask directly about the reason for their failure to drive out the demon, and Jesus identifies their lack of prayer as the problem (Mark 9:28-29). In Matthew's account, Jesus emphasizes their lack of faith as the fundamental problem (Matthew 17:20). In the end, it seems that both the larger crowd and the Twelve in particular are guilty of lacking faith.

The good news is, however, that Jesus' power and authority are not limited by any human weakness or failing, not even by our lack of faith. And despite the demon's last-ditch efforts to afflict the child (Luke **9:42**), Jesus rebukes the evil spirit (see 4:35), heals the child's body (see Luke 8:54-55), and restores the boy to his father (see Luke 7:15). In a powerful picture of redemption, Jesus has put back in order all of the chaos and brokenness in this family's life.

This account presses home the need for faith. In this particular case, faith is confidence in Jesus' power and authority to help us. It

> The good news is that Jesus' power is not limited by human weakness or failing.

is normally pretty easy to trust Jesus when things are going well. We might even find faith close at hand when we need to trust Jesus with a problem, so long as a reasonable solution is apparent and likely. But it is circumstances like this one that really reveal the degree to which we trust Jesus' wisdom, timing, love and power. When the disease is not cured, when the job offer does not materialize, when the relationship is not reconciled—in those cases we see what (or who) it is that we really trust.

Thankfully, we do not have to earn Jesus' love and help through our faith. It is not as if Jesus is waiting for us to clear a certain bar of faith, at which point he will come and intervene in our problems. Instead, when we come to him, he even helps us with our ongoing struggle with lingering disbelief. We can cry out, like this boy's father, "I do believe; help me overcome my unbelief!" (Mark 9:24).

True Greatness

In response to the healing of the child, Luke tells us "they were all amazed at the greatness of God" (Luke **9:43**). While the three disciples got a glimpse of the majesty of Jesus at the transfiguration, the people down below got a glimpse of that same glory at work in his victory over demonic forces. You can imagine the excitement in the crowd; Jesus has just waltzed in to an intractable situation and accomplished the seemingly impossible. Perhaps that is why the disciples are arguing about who is going to be the greatest (**v 46**). It seems that Jesus' incredible display of greatness has whetted their appetite for the coming of his kingdom; naturally they begin to wonder about their own relative place in it. Each of them wants to be well positioned for a place of power when Jesus finally turns his marvelous power on the occupying Roman forces.

But Jesus acted immediately to crush their misguided aspirations. While they were still marveling, he pulled his disciples aside for a lesson. Warning them to pay careful attention, he explained for the second time that the Son of Man was going to be "delivered into the hands of men" (**v 44**, see v 22). The adoration of the crowds would not last; the fickle hearts of men would betray him and send him to his death. The irony is thick here: while the disciples (insignificant in every way) were thinking about their own future grandeur, Jesus (the truly glorious one) was thinking about his upcoming suffering. In light of that disconnect, it is easy to understand why the disciples failed to understand Jesus' meaning (**v 45**).

But because Jesus knew their thoughts, he made an object lesson of a child who must have been nearby (**v 47**), saying, in effect, *This is greatness in my kingdom*. If the disciples are willing to embrace and receive a child in his name—that is, for Jesus' sake—they will be receiving Jesus himself. And if they receive Jesus, they will have received the Father, who sent him (**v 48**).

The point is not, as some have suggested, that Jesus is saying that there's something inherently great about children. Instead, Jesus is taking the child as an example of someone who has very little that would seem great. A child has no power, no money, no recognition or accomplishments. It's easy to be kind to the rich and powerful; they can bless you back (see 6:33). But Jesus is calling his disciples to imitate him by showing love to even the very least.

In that imitation, we find a definition for true greatness. It is hard for us, because most of us are not content to pursue holiness by humble, self-giving love for the lowly. Most of us not only want to be great but we also want to be *perceived* as great by others. Like the disciples, we want to be great in comparison to others—to be the greatest. Think about how ridiculous this scenario is: it's not enough for them that they were in the enviable position of being part of the Messiah's inner circle. You might think they would be content with that much greatness, but their hearts won't settle until they are recognized as the greatest of the inner circle. They even go so far as to try and get Jesus to stop someone from outside their group of twelve who is trying to minister in Jesus' name (**9:49-50**)!

Notice that Jesus doesn't necessarily attack the human impulse to achieve greatness. Instead he redefines it so that we can see what it really means to be great; that is, greatness as God sees it. It is a call to humility and service; it is a call to love what Jesus loves and do what Jesus does (see Mark 10:43-44). Already in Luke's Gospel, the people who have been held up as models of true greatness (the "heroes," if you will) have been the marginalized and insignificant: a woman with a bad reputation, a pregnant virgin, a tax collector, an unclean woman. The people who seem great in the eyes of the world are not necessarily perceived in the same way by the King of God's kingdom.

If you are going to follow a crucified Messiah, a Son of Man who was delivered over to the hands of men, then you are going to have to accept that genuine greatness is going to look different than you might naturally think. At this moment in time, the world around us tells us to measure personal worth in terms of physical appearance, material possessions, professional or academic accomplishments, or even our social-media presence. Those are **barometers** of significance that can be understood, quantified, and diligently sought after. But Jesus is saying here that the truly great one is the one who is willing to humbly love the "insignificant" person for Jesus' sake. Perhaps the greatest person in your church is not the pastor who preaches the brilliant sermon that everyone appreci-

> If you are going to follow a crucified Messiah, genuine greatness is going to look different.

ates, but the "ordinary" member who is willing to drive 15 minutes out of her way to pick up an elderly person who cannot get to the church meeting on her own. The way to find life is to deny yourself (Luke 9:23); the way to save your life is to lose it (v 24).

How can it be that we who know the sacrificial love of Christ so often have the greasy fingerprints of pride all over our lives? Why is it that we are so easily offended, so quick to anger when we don't get our way, so slow to serve those who cannot do anything for us? In light of Jesus' sacrifice, it should be inconceivable that a Christian would be consumed by a passion for his or her own glory, but the disciples' tone-deaf argument about their own personal greatness reminds us that pride is a foe that we need to battle every day by looking to Jesus and his death for us. The words that Isaac Watts penned three hundred years ago remain the prayer of every Christian:

When I survey the wondrous cross
On which the Prince of glory died,
My richest gain I count but loss,
And pour contempt on all my pride.

Questions for reflection

1. About which part of your life do you need to cry out to Jesus, "I do believe; help me in my unbelief"?

2. Has this section caused you to consider your view of what makes someone great?

3. Who are the "little children" who you are being called to welcome, love and serve? What might stop you doing that?

10. ON THE ROAD TO JERUSALEM

We now reach a major transition point in Luke's Gospel. Jesus has twice told his disciples that he is going to die (9:22, 44) and he has discussed his upcoming "exodus" in Jerusalem with Moses and Elijah on the mountain (v 31). But now "the time approached for him to be taken up to heaven" and so "Jesus resolutely set out for Jerusalem" (**v 51**). From this point on, we will see fewer miracles, fewer extended blocks of public teaching, and fewer crowds, as the narrative drives toward the climax of Jesus' crucifixion, resurrection, and ascension into heaven.

In order to understand the events that are about to take place in Jerusalem, we must have firmly fixed in our mind that Jesus understood that he had been sent by his heavenly Father (**10:16**, though we have already been alerted to this fact back in 4:18). He was not a rogue agent; he was not making up the terms of his mission as he went along. Instead, he had been sent to accomplish a specific task: namely, dying on the cross and rising from the dead for the salvation of his people. This is why Jesus spoke in terms of his suffering as something that must take place (see 9:22); it was necessary because the Father had sent him to do it. For that reason, it is significant that Jesus chooses to send his followers out repeatedly in this passage.

What (Not) to Do in the Face of Rejection

Up until this point most of the action has taken place in the region of Galilee, up in the north. For Jesus to head from Galilee to Jerusalem in the south without a long detour, he would be required to pass through the land of the **Samaritans**. Relations between Jews and Samaritans were frosty at best, and Jewish travelers were often harassed as they passed through on their way to or from Jerusalem. So when Jesus sent disciples ahead to a Samaritan village to prepare for his arrival, it is not surprising that they did not warmly receive a Jewish rabbi on his way to Jerusalem (**v 52-53**).

James and John did not take this insult to their master lightly. The brothers, whom Jesus had nicknamed "sons of thunder" (see Mark 3:17), offered to show off their new-found spiritual authority by calling down heavenly fire on the offending village (Luke **9:54**). While that might seem harsh to us, and it certainly was, it was not without an Old Testament precedent. In the book of 2 Kings, we read about a time when the prophet Elijah proved that he was a legitimate prophet by calling down fire from heaven on a group of Samaritan soldiers (2 Kings 1:1-12). The disciples' offer may well have been rooted in an assumption that Jesus would want to make a similar demonstration of his legitimacy in the face of Samaritan rejection.

But it is clear from Jesus' rebuke (Luke **9:55**) that the two brothers have badly misunderstood the nature of Jesus' mission. He has come to save those who reject him by dying in their place, a fact that is driven home by Luke in the book of Acts when the Samaritans become some of the first people to embrace the gospel (Acts 8:1-25). In the face of rejection, Jesus and his disciples simply move on to the next village (Luke **9:56**).

This is not to say that judgment has no place in Jesus' ministry. His instructions to his disciples in **10:10-12** make it clear that rejecting the message of the kingdom has terrible consequences. Wiping dust from one's feet was a custom that Jews employed to communicate their disdain when leaving a Gentile region; it was a "warning" sign of rejection and condemnation (**v 11**). When a town rejected the disciples that Jesus had sent, they were rejecting both him and the Father who sent him (**v 16**), an action that would surely have consequences in the long term.

Jesus then enters into a series of shocking statements about the final day of judgment (**v 12-15**), saying that on that day famous Old Testament objects of wrath like **Sodom, Tyre, and Sidon** will fare better than the Jewish town where Jesus had performed many of his miracles. The kingdom had come near to these cities (**v 11**) and so rejecting such a message was worse than even the worst Gentile perversion. The important lesson is that judgment will most certainly come to all who reject Jesus, but it is not the disciples' responsibility to make that judgment happen. The sent ones take the news of the kingdom around but judgment is left to God and his timing.

This is a helpful reminder to Christians. We still live in the era before the final judgment. Now is the time for us to be sent around the world with the good news that God's salvation has come in the person of Jesus. And so, while we may be rightly upset when we see the ever-increasing hostility of the world around to our Jesus, we are not authorized to execute judgment. We are sent to preach the gospel message (including the warning that a day of reckoning is most certainly coming), and we leave the judgment up to God for when he sees fit.

Seventy-Two Sent

After the experience in Samaria, Jesus sends ahead a group of seventy-two disciples. Their job is to heal the sick and declare the nearness of the kingdom (**v 9**) to people in light of Jesus' imminent arrival in their town (**v 1**). Even this larger workforce is not nearly sufficient for the task of spreading the message, and so the disciples are encouraged to "ask the Lord of the harvest, therefore, to send out workers into his harvest field" (**v 2**).

Next, Jesus gives them instructions on how to go about their mission. With the day of judgment looming in the future, the task of spreading the message is extremely urgent. The sent ones cannot afford to carry extra luggage; they will have to rely on the Lord's provision; there is no time for the sent ones to stop and chat along the road (**v 4**).

To receive a messenger of the kingdom is akin to receiving the King himself (**v 16**). The disciple comes as an ambassador of peace (**v 5**); if he receives a peace-filled welcome in a house, peace will rest on that household (**v 6**). They can stay in one home and eat and drink with a clear conscience, for the blessing they bring is far more valuable than the cost of their support (**v 7-8**).

Jesus' instructions here are not meant as a step-by-step manual for an approach to modern missions; these are instructions for a specific place and time. So we cannot conclude that it is disobedient for a missionary to bring a bag with her. She is not required to find someone who promotes peace and stay with that person. Instead, we must take to heart the urgency of the task of spreading the message of salvation. Whether we are **vocational missionaries** to a foreign culture or merely missionaries to our workplaces and our children, the task is urgent. It should lead us to pray and to proclaim the good news.

The Cause of Our Joy

Given the difficult circumstances into which these few "lambs" had been sent (**v 3**), we might expect that they would have come back battered and bruised, with their tails between their legs. But instead of encountering defeat and discouragement, they had experienced an unanticipated provision of power: "Even the demons submit to us in your name" (**v 17**). As a result, they "returned with joy."

Jesus had just warned Capernaum that instead of being exalted into heaven, they would be cast down into Hades (**v 15**), an image that calls to mind the judgment on the king of Babylon celebrated in Isaiah 14:13-15. Now Jesus applies the picture to Satan, whom Jesus saw fall "like lightning from heaven" when the kingdom of God invaded the world (Luke **10:18**). Unbeknown to the disciples, their ministry of proclamation and healing and casting out demons sent shockwaves through the unseen spiritual realm. None of this is to be attributed to the power of the disciples; Jesus is the one who has given them authority "to overcome all the power of the enemy" (**v 19**).

The joy of the disciples is easy to understand. Who would not be excited to see such a display of God's power? Jesus encourages their joy, but locates it on a different foundation: "Rejoice that your names are written in heaven" (**v 20**). It is a tremendous blessing to see the Lord working through you; growth in holiness and fruitfulness in ministry are good reasons to be thankful to God. But God has an even greater blessing for his people, for he has written their names in heaven. That is to say, he has brought us into an unshakeable relationship with himself that will be fully realized in the joy of heaven.

This is a great reminder to all believers not to put our hope in our service to God and the way that he may choose to use us. Seasons of fruitfulness may come and go, and in any case the Lord will raise up other laborers after we are gone. If our identity and happiness is wrapped up in those things, we will despair. But we have a better source of joy; the promise of heaven has no peaks or valleys and the joy of belonging to the Lord knows no season. These disciples were truly most blessed; they had an incredible cause for joy, for they were seeing and hearing things to which even "prophets and kings" did not have access (**v 23-24**).

The Cause of Jesus' Joy

What follows next is, says Edwards, "the most exultant description of Jesus in all Scripture" (*The Gospel According to Luke*, page 313). Jesus was "full of joy" through the Spirit. B.B. Warfield commented that,

> "the word is a strong one and conveys the idea of exuberant gladness, a gladness which fills the heart."
>
> (*The Emotional Life of our Lord*, page 123)

In other words, Jesus is overflowingly joyful at the reality of his disciples' salvation (**v 21**). Not only were their names written in heaven but the Father was accomplishing their salvation in a way that confounded the "wise and learned" and instead gave the blessings to the simple and meek. Instead of showering his grace on the religious leaders and respectable people, God was bringing into his kingdom the spiritual equivalent of "little children"—the immoral tax collectors and uneducated fishermen.

And all of this was due to the sovereign pleasure of the Father and the Son to whom he has committed "all things" (**v 22**). The only way to come to know the Father in a saving and joy-producing way is to have him revealed to you by the choice of the Son.

The joy of the kingdom comes with a cost. While on the road, Jesus had three interactions with people who expressed a desire to follow him (**9:57-62**). Instead of being grateful for their interest and warmly welcoming them into the fold, Jesus warned them that membership in the kingdom must take precedence even over important social customs like performing burial rites for the dead (**v 59-60**) and other family obligations (**v 61-62**). In a sense, Jesus is putting flesh on what it means to pick up one's cross and follow him.

> 100% of the costs of the kingdom are incurred in the temporal realm—none in the eternal one.

But even though there is a cost, the kingdom is not ultimately about struggle and difficulty. While we can speak of Jesus as a "man of suffering, and familiar with pain" (Isaiah 53:3), he was not a dour or unpleasant person to be around. Honoring his Father by accomplishing our salvation brought him exceeding joy. The salvation that he brings is a matter of great joy for us (see Luke 2:10) and for him (Hebrews 12:2) and for the Father (Luke **10:21**). While we have been reminded repeatedly in Luke's Gospel that following Christ is costly, we must remember that 100% of the costs are incurred in the **temporal realm**—none are borne in the eternal one. The costs are far outstripped by the never-ending joy that belongs to those whose names are written in heaven.

Questions for reflection

1. Would you say you are too quick to wish God's judgment on those who treat you (or him) badly, or too slow to speak about his judgment at all, or both?

2. Have you experienced both the ups and downs of Christian ministry? How did you react emotionally, and what does that suggest about the place of ministry in your identity?

3. In reality, what is your greatest source of joy? How would meditating on the truth that your name is "written in heaven" relocate your joy-source?

PART TWO

Luke moves on to record for us a conversation between Jesus and a religious leader referred to as "an expert in the law" (**v 25**). We are tipped off at the outset that his motives are not pure and his question is not an honest one. But even though his intention is to test Jesus, his question was an important one: "What must I do to inherit eternal life?" The wording of the question implies that he is looking for one specific act that he can perform that will give him the key to eternal life.

But as he so often did, Jesus quickly and effortlessly flips the script. The lawyer has come to trap Jesus, but with a single quick question from Jesus the expert finds himself on the back foot. Instead of answering the question, Jesus puts it back to him: based on his extensive knowledge of the law, what needs to be done (**v 26**)? The man's answer (**v 27**) is a combination of Deuteronomy 6:5 and Leviticus 19:18: the law demands both that we love God with everything we have and that we love our neighbor as we love ourselves. We might expect that Jesus would verbally **eviscerate** this insincere questioner, but surprisingly he indicates his approval of the man's answer (**v 28**, see Matthew 22:34-40). It will soon become evident, however, that the terms of the commandment need to be defined carefully.

The Wrong Question

At this point, the lawyer should just cut his losses. He has stood up to test the teacher, perhaps hoping that Jesus would say something controversial about the Law of Moses. But Jesus has played it straight, affirming an **orthodox** application of the two greatest commandments. There will be no theological fireworks today.

Now the question lingers in the air: has he really met the requirements of the law? Could anyone honestly say that they have cleared the bar of whole-hearted, total-soul, complete-strength, all-mind love for God? Jesus did not simply affirm the man's theology; he instructed him to actually do what the law commanded in order to live (Luke **10:28**).

But this man was controlled by a desire to justify himself, and so he asked exactly the wrong follow-up question. He should have asked, "How can someone find eternal life if they have failed to love God and his neighbor perfectly?" In that case Jesus would have responded with the good news that he had not come for the righteous and spiritually healthy, but for those sinners who knew they were in need of a physician for their souls (see Luke 5:31-32).

However, this teacher of the law did not want Jesus to justify him. Instead, he wanted to justify himself (**10:29**); he wanted to be right with God on his own merits. And so he sought to do what eve-

> Every works-based religion must lower God's standards to a place where they can be cleared by means of human effort.

ryone operating within a **works-based religion** must do—try to lower God's standards down to a place where they can be cleared by means of human effort.

In that light, the man's request for clarification seems like an effort to limit the law's demands. If eternal life requires him to love his neighbor, then how tightly can he draw the circle of people to whom he owes that kind of love? Perhaps if he can define the terms of the law narrowly, he will be able to do the things necessary to inherit eternal life.

The Story

The story that Jesus tells the man is well known to us, but it is hard for us to appreciate exactly how shocking it would have been to this lawyer. We're told that a man was walking down from Jerusalem to Jericho, a treacherous but commercially important route. This was a winding seventeen-mile journey through limestone crags, descending 3,400 feet (1,036 metres) to 800 feet (244 metres) below sea level. Numerous caves along the route provided a perfect place for thieves and robbers to hide, and as a result this route was famously dangerous. In fact, most people would not have attempted the journey alone.

Thus, when Jesus begins his parable with the words, "A man was going down from Jerusalem to Jericho" (**v 30**), the stomach of every listener would have tightened. It is like saying, "A man walked down a dark alley alone." Everyone would be able to guess what happens next: the man is going to be robbed and beaten, which is precisely what happens.

But the attack is not really the important part of the story. We are not told anything about the man, whether he was rich or poor, good or bad. We are not even told anything about the robbers. Instead the central actors, the ones from whom we are supposed to learn, are the three passers-by. Initially the victimized man seems to have a bit of good fortune, for a priest happens along the road (**v 31**). This is not a far-fetched development, for many priests lived in Jericho and would use this road to return home after their temple service was complete in the capital city. But our hopes are quickly dashed as the priest passes by without aiding the man in distress. In the same way, a Levite comes and goes without helping (**v 32**).

It is easy to condemn these two men as heartless, but their behavior was not completely without explanation. After all, this was obviously not a safe place to stop. The man lying there in a pool of his own blood was proof positive that there were dangerous people in the area. In addition, the beaten man may have looked as if he was already dead (Jesus says that he was left "half-dead" in **verse 30**). If he were dead, then touching him would not help him but would result in ceremonial uncleanness for the priest and Levite. And finally, they did not know if they had any obligation to this man; he was not family and they didn't even know if he was a Jew. So perhaps the smart decision was to simply keep moving along the road.

The third person to come along the road was a Samaritan (**v 33**). We have already experienced a taste of the tension that existed between the Jews and the Samaritans. For a Jew, Samaritans were the kind of people on whom you hoped fire from heaven would fall (see 9:51-56). In the ears of Jesus' audience, he would have been roughly like an Islamic extremist operative would be to someone in the West. Surely this is going to be the villain in the story.

But instead, he "took pity on him" (**10:33**) and lavished kindness on the wounded stranger at his own personal expense. Despite the potential danger, he pulled out oil and wine and attended to the man's injuries (**v 34**). Laying the man on his donkey meant that he had to walk the rest of the way to the inn, and once they arrived there, the Samaritan spent his time and a considerable amount of money making sure that the man's needs were provided for (**v 35**). The man's kindness is extravagant; the fact that he is a Samaritan makes the story scandalous.

The Question That is the Answer

That parable constitutes Jesus' answer to the religious leader's question. He wanted to know how narrowly he could construe his obligation and still please God, and so he had asked, "Who is my neighbor?" But in the end all that he gets from Jesus is a question to answer: "Which of these three do you think was a neighbor to the man who fell into the hands of robbers?" (**v 36**). Jesus has effectively reframed the discussion by asking the question that the teacher of the law should have asked. Instead of asking, "Who am I required to love?" the question he should have been asking is, "To whom can I be a loving neighbor?"

Jesus' closing words drive home the point: "Go and do likewise" (**v 37**). Love for one's neighbor requires us to imitate the Samaritan in his extravagant, costly, self-sacrificing, culture-crossing love. Followers of Jesus are called to show love for anyone in need, even if that person would consider us an enemy (see 6:27). Tim Keller summarizes the point well:

"We instinctively tend to limit for whom we exert ourselves. We do it for people like us, and for people whom we like. Jesus will have none of that. By depicting a Samaritan helping a Jew, Jesus could not have found a more forceful way to say that anyone at all in need—regardless of race, politics, class, and religion—is your neighbor. Not everyone is your brother or sister in faith, but everyone is your neighbor, and you must love your neighbor."

(*Generous Justice*, pages 67-68)

The Real Good Samaritan

This whole incident began with a man asking how he could inherit eternal life. But in the end, he wanted to know how he could earn it by his obedience to the law. After Jesus defined his obligation to neighbor-love in the broadest terms, an unasked question lingers in the air: Do you still want to depend on your obedience to the law? Are you still interested in justifying yourself? Or are you now ready to admit that you cannot earn eternal life by your religious performance?

In the end, we do not understand Jesus' parable until we put ourselves in the proper place in the story. We tend to read it as if we are only meant to find ourselves in the people who pass by the helpless man. In that case, the most important question remains: will you show love or will you ignore the needs in front of you? As we have seen, that is an important question for us to ask as followers of Jesus.

But when we step back and look at the bigger picture, we see that we actually bear more spiritual resemblance to the helpless man dying by the side of the road than to the Samaritan. Unless someone comes to rescue him with sacrificial neighbor-love, he will certainly perish. In the same way, we are in desperate need of someone to show love to us in our sin-sick condition.

From that perspective, we can see that Jesus is the true Good Samaritan. He came to us while we were still his enemies; he met us when we were dead in our sins and trespasses. He fulfilled the requirements and paid the price so that our soul's wounds might be healed.

It is only by trusting in Christ's death and resurrection for us that we can inherit eternal life.

Once we have understood that truth, we will find that we are able to truly extend ourselves in love to those in physical and spiritual need around us. A heart that has been touched by the unmerited love of Christ will be moved to show that love to others who may not deserve it. Jesus has loved you; go and do likewise!

Questions for reflection

1. The expert in the law tried to lower God's standards down to a place where they could be cleared by means of human effort. Are you ever tempted to do this, so that you can view God's ongoing love for you as earned by you in some way? How do you do this?

2. As you read the parable with yourself in the role of a passer-by, how are you challenged?

3. As you read the parable with yourselves in the role of the injured man and the Lord as the Samaritan, how are you thrilled?

11. LISTENING AND SPEAKING

What does Jesus most want from us? And how does God want us to speak to him? Those are the questions which the next two conversations that Luke sets before us address, and in both cases we ought not to let familiarity with famous passages dilute the surprises and the excitements.

Jesus has previously sent his disciples ahead of him in preparation for his arrival (10:1-7), and now Luke tells us the story of two women who extended a warm welcome to him (**v 38**).

Jesus, as was his custom, would have sat down and begun to teach, and Mary "sat at the Lord's feet" (**v 39**), while her sister Martha "was distracted by all the preparations that had to be made" (**v 40**). Martha was understandably upset about the inequitable distribution of chores, and so she appealed to Jesus to intervene in order to make her sister do her fair share of the work. One of these sisters has invested all of her energies in making sure that she can hear Jesus teach, while the other has invested all her energies into serving Jesus and meeting his needs. Which one has her priorities in the right place?

Jesus' answer might surprise us: Martha has opened her home to Jesus, and busied herself with "much serving" (**v 40**,). Mary, on the other hand, is merely sitting there listening to Jesus. It seems that Martha should be the one in line for Jesus' commendation; she certainly thought so! But instead Jesus corrects her gently in **verses 41-42**: "You are worried and upset about many things, but few things are needed—or indeed only one. Mary has chosen what is better, and it will not be taken away from her." Martha is confused about who is the one truly spreading the feast in her home. If she would only stop for a moment, she would see that Jesus really wants to serve her with his teaching.

Many Christians spend their days running around, anxious and troubled, consumed with the things that they have to get done. After all, life presents a seemingly unlimited array of opportunities to be busy and harried with the stresses of daily life. But the one thing most necessary in our lives is to invest our time in listening to Jesus' teaching. As with any other relationship, our relationship with Jesus is based on spending time with him. We do that not primarily by serving him but by getting to know him through his word. Clean houses and full bank accounts will not endure past the grave, but our relationship with Jesus through his words now, and face to face one day, can never be taken from us (**v 42**).

This short story of Mary and Martha helps us to be prepared for what is about to come in Luke's Gospel. The disciples' request in **11:1** illustrates what we might call "the Mary principle"; they want more of his teaching! Specifically, they ask Jesus to instruct them on the topic of prayer. It seems that John the Baptist had given his followers some instruction about the mechanics of prayer, and here Jesus' disciples want access to the secrets of their master's prayer life. In response Jesus gives them a model for prayer.

A Holy Name

When we look carefully at the prayer, we see that it is broken down into five requests made to God. First, Jesus teaches the disciples to pray that God the Father's name would be hallowed (**v 2**). "Hallowed" simply means "holy"; the request is that the name of God would be recognized and considered holy. In the Bible, a person's name includes his reputation and all that is said about him. God's name stands for all that he is, and so Jesus teaches us to pray that it would be hallowed.

And it is important to recognize that Jesus is not teaching us to tell God in prayer that his name is holy. This is a request, not a statement about what is already true. When we pray, "Hallowed be your name," we are asking God to make the world honor his name as holy. It is a way of making God's glory and fame our highest priority. We are asking him to do whatever is necessary to make his holiness known and cherished throughout the world. There is a temptation to think of prayer as fundamentally our going to

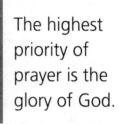

The highest priority of prayer is the glory of God.

God for the stuff that we want and need. And Jesus does makes it clear in **verse 3** that it is appropriate to ask God for our material needs, but this first petition shows us that the highest priority of prayer is the glory of God.

Have you ever wondered why we need to pray? After all, God does not need to be informed of our needs; he knows them far better than we do. Instead, prayer is most basically about God's glory. Everything else that Jesus will teach us about prayer has to be understood in this context. When we pray, we are asking God to make himself known and glorious by providing for his people and forgiving their sins and delivering them from temptation.

A Coming Kingdom

The second petition is simply "Your kingdom come" (**v 2**), a prayer for what Bock calls "the full realization and culmination of God's promised rule" (*Luke 9:51–24:53*, page 1053). When we ask God to make his kingdom come, we are imploring him to rule over us so that his kingdom's purposes are accomplished in everything great and small. It is essentially the prayer that "your will be done, on earth as it is in heaven" (see Matthew 6:10). This is a prayer that Jesus' disciples will continue to pray until he returns and fully establishes his kingdom.

Our Daily Bread

The next request is that God would "give us each day our daily bread" (Luke **11:3**). Jesus switches to the present tense in this verse; we are to ask God for the things we require on a regular basis because we are in need of God's provision daily. The phrase calls to mind the experience of Israel in the wilderness, where the Lord miraculously provided manna each morning. God has proven that he can and will care for his people's practical needs and so Jesus encourages us to ask him for it.

In an economic environment like that of first-century Palestine, many people did not have vast stores of food to count on. They were quite literally in need of bread daily, an experience that is foreign to many of us now. But our stocked pantries do not mean that we are somehow less dependent every day on God than people were in Jesus' day. Instead, it is likely that we are simply less aware of our need than people were in Jesus' day. Supermarkets full of food, and large houses, and the developments of modern medicine can serve to dull our sense of dependence on God. Oftentimes it is only when a crisis hits that we feel acutely how dependent we are on God, and only then do we pray. But it should not be so; Jesus encourages us to go to God daily, acknowledging our dependence on him and asking for his provision.

Our Sins Forgiven

The fourth request is that God would "forgive us our sins" (**v 4**). Jesus' followers are acutely aware of their failures and shortcomings (see 6:41), and so they know that they must appeal to God for forgiveness. It is perhaps a more subtle need, but we require this daily mercy from God every bit as much as we need him to give us our daily bread.

If we hope to experience God's forgiveness, we should be willing to extend forgiveness to "everyone who sins against us." Jesus isn't suggesting that God should be expected to forgive us only to the extent that we have forgiven other people who have sinned against us. None of us are so forgiving that we can merit God's patience and grace. Instead, Jesus is making an argument from the lesser to the greater. Since even sinful people like you and me forgive others, we can confidently ask a merciful God for forgiveness. But equally, if we do not forgive others, we show that we have not really received forgiveness from God—for if we have experienced that greater forgiveness, we will display the lesser forgiveness (however hard or costly that may be) to those around us.

Help in Temptation

The final request in Jesus' prayer is a petition for spiritual protection, that God would "lead us not into temptation" (**11:4**). The wording might make it seem that we are supposed to ask God to kindly refrain from trying to trip us up with temptation to sin, but we know in fact that God never tempts anyone (James 1:13). Instead, Jesus is encouraging us to express an attitude that acknowledges that we need God's help and protection in times of temptation (see Paul's words in 1 Corinthians 10:13).

A User's Guide

A question that Christians have asked is: how should we use this prayer? Is it meant to be something that we repeat **verbatim**, as the substance of our prayers? Or should we understand it as simply a model for prayer, showing us what kinds of things we should take to the Lord in prayer?

The answer is most likely "both." Jesus seems to have expected that the disciples would have repeated this prayer verbatim, for he introduces his teaching with the instructions, "When you pray, say..." (Luke **11:2**). So it is certainly appropriate for us to pray these exact words, especially in the worship of the local church (notice that this is a corporate prayer—"forgive us our sins").

In Matthew's Gospel the prayer comes in the context of a warning about the mindlessly repetitive prayers of the **pagans,** and there Jesus frames his teaching in terms of the manner in which his followers ought to pray: "This, then, is how you should pray" (Matthew 6:9). But we can also use Jesus' teaching here to inform us about the priorities that should shape our prayers. Godly prayer is not merely a grown-up version of a child's Christmas list for Santa, but a plea for God's glory to be spread, and for his grace and mercy to be made manifest in our lives.

The Motivation for Prayer

It's one thing to know how to pray, but having the motivation to pray is another thing altogether. Many Christians have been taught how to pray, but for some reason they just do not do it all that often. And so Jesus follows up his teaching on how to pray by helping us to see why we ought to pray in the first place, beginning with the fact that God is our Father. The centuries have diluted the shock of Jesus' address in the Lord's Prayer, but it was not at all normal for a first-century Jew to call God "Father" (see John 5:18). But not only does Jesus call God his Father; he instructs us to do so as well (Luke **11:2**).

We ought to be motivated to pray by the fact that God is our loving Father. The importance of this fact for our prayer life is immediately apparent, for human fathers want the best for their children. Fathers do not withhold good things from their children; no dad would respond to a request for food with something harmful or dangerous (**v 11-12**). If that's the case among human fathers, who are prone to sin and weakness, how much more can we be certain that God will give us every good thing that we need when we ask him for it (**v 13**)? It is significant that Jesus introduces the gift of the Holy Spirit here (**v 13**), for this is the greatest gift of all, and it is one that many of God's children aren't even aware that they should be asking for. We might say that when God's children ask him for help (or ask for the wrong things!), he gives them the very best gifts—or, perhaps, the very best *gift*, singular.

The story about the friend who arrives at midnight (**v 5-8**) illustrates the way that this works. While the story is a bit strange to our modern ears, the point is fairly simple. Imagine if your neighbor woke you up at midnight to borrow a cup of sugar. You would probably be fairly annoyed, but you would probably also give them the sugar they asked for. The sheer audacity of the request is what causes it to succeed. In the same way, the friend doesn't give his neighbor the bread he seeks out of the goodness of his heart, but rather, because he has been asked with **impudence** (**v 8**).

And if audacious asking brings results in the realm of human friendship, how much more so when it comes to our heavenly Father? He is never annoyed or impatient when we come to him with our needs. So when we knock on the door of heaven in prayer, we find it opened for us. When we seek the help of our heavenly Father, we find it. When we ask in prayer for the help that we need, we are sure to receive it (**v 9-10**).

If you do not pray much, perhaps you do not take seriously the fact that God is your heavenly Father. Or perhaps you think that God is not willing to hear your prayers. Maybe deep down you believe that it does not matter whether you ask or not. But let Jesus' words here encourage you to pray right now; your Father is ready to hear you and bless you.

Questions for reflection

1. Does your daily routine show that you agree with Jesus that "only one" thing is truly necessary each day, and what that thing is; or does it suggest that you don't believe him?

2. Why is it liberating to know that the only thing that the Lord says we "must" do each day is relate to and spend time with him?

3. How has 11:1-13 helped you *want* to pray, and helped you with *what* to pray?

PART TWO

Luke transitions away from the theme of prayer abruptly and we now turn our focus to Jesus, much to everyone's astonishment, casting out a demon that was causing a man to be mute (**v 14**). This put some of the bystanders (namely, the Pharisees, according to Matthew 9:32-34) in a difficult position. They didn't like Jesus, to put it mildly. But they could not deny his power to heal and cast out demons, and it is really difficult to compete for people's respect with a man who can cast out demons. So their preferred course of action is to attribute Jesus' extraordinary powers to the workings of the devil.

A Kingdom Divided

They alleged that "by Beelzebul, the prince of demons, he is driving out demons" (Luke **11:15**). While there's nothing in the Bible confirming the existence of a demon named Beelzebul, it was a common notion in Jesus' day. The name means "Lord of the flies" and comes from the name of a **Canaanite** god. By linking Jesus' power to the realm of demons, they seek to discredit that which they cannot deny. Their plan is perfect—except for the fact that it makes no sense at all.

Jesus "knew their thoughts," and bluntly points out the failure in their logic: "Any kingdom divided against itself will be ruined, and a house divided against itself will fall" (**v 17**). Satan is a murderer and destroyer; he loves to spread misery and suffering. His demons possessed people and made them miserable. Jesus, on the other hand, came healing and reviving. He brought joy and forgiveness; he cast out demons and brought relief to those that suffer. Given that, how exactly does it make any sense to attribute the actions of Jesus to demonic power? Why would Satan empower Jesus to fight against him? What ruler would divide his kingdom against itself (**v 18**)?

Jesus presses the point further there in **verse 19**: "If I drive out demons by Beelzebul, by whom do your [the Pharisees'] followers [literally, "your sons"] drive them out?" If Jesus is working through the power of Satan, as his opponents claim, then so must the Pharisees! No—what his opponents consider to be evidence of satanic activity is actually proof that "the kingdom of God has come upon you" (**11:20**).

Jesus uses a simple illustration to help his hearers understand his relationship to the demonic forces at work in their world (**v 21-22**). Satan is like a strong man with a lot of treasure, guarding his house without fear. People are like his "possessions"; they are enslaved to sin and oppressed by demons. As long as no one stronger than the devil comes along, they will never be delivered. But when someone stronger than the strong man comes and attacks, then the treasures of his house can be liberated.

You can imagine the crowd's collective jaw dropping here. Jesus is claiming that he is the one who has the power (see 3:16) to walk into the devil's house and take his stuff. Satan has been in control on earth (albeit in a **provisional** way) up until this point, but now that the kingdom of God has come, he has been overpowered. That's the true explanation for what Jesus is doing when he casts demons out of people.

Life looks a lot different when you view it through the lens of what Jesus is saying here. No matter how wise, beautiful, or wealthy someone may be, apart from Jesus that person is a captive of the devil, in desperate need of rescue. And so followers of Christ should be humble, grateful people. On one hand we might be tempted to think highly of ourselves; on the other hand we might be jealous of others who seem to have much more talent and confidence than we do. But the ground is level at the foot of the cross; if we were left to our own devices, we would all still be Satan's captives. If we really take to heart the truth of this passage, there is no room for either pride or fear of man, but just gratitude to Jesus!

You Have to Choose

Luke tells us that the crowd was split regarding Jesus' ministry. Some opposed him and accused him of working by the power of Satan (**11:15**), but others were more open-minded. These people were respectably **agnostic**; they wanted more information. And so, after seeing Jesus cast out a demon, they asked (apparently without a sense of irony) for Jesus to show them a sign (**v 16**).

When Jesus finally gets around to addressing their request, he tells them that while their desire for a sign might seem like open-minded neutrality, it is actually evidence that they are wicked (**v 29**). As such, they will receive no sign "except the sign of Jonah. For as Jonah was a sign to the Ninevites, so also will the Son of Man be to this generation" (**v 29-30**). Just as Jonah preached God's message to the ancient people of Nineveh, in the same way Jesus was God's messenger to the crowds of his day. (For more detail of potential interpretations of "the sign of Jonah" here, see Bock, *Luke 9:51–24:53*, pages 1096-1098.)

> When it comes to Jesus, there are no neutral people and there is no middle ground.

If the wicked Ninevites repented at Jonah's preaching, why could these people not see what was required of them now that "something greater than Jonah" had arrived (**v 32**)? If the pagan Queen of the South traveled to learn from Solomon (see 1 Kings 10:1-5), how much worse would it be for them if they failed to respond to one greater than Solomon (Luke **11:31**)? There will be judgment for those who hear the messenger and reject him. Signs and miracles and exorcisms are great, but spiritually speaking, the most important thing is that we hear the word of God and keep it (**v 27-28**).

Since that is the case, when it comes to Jesus there are no neutral people and there is no middle ground—"Whoever is not with me is against me, and whoever does not gather with me scatters" (**v 23**). Lots of choices in our lives are trivial and therefore unimportant, but when it comes to the Son of Man there cannot possibly be a middle ground. Either he is the strong man who has come to bind the devil, or he is working by the power of Beelzebul. If you are not for him, you are against him by default.

Jesus illustrates the principle there in **verses 24-26**. And while there are confusing details that could potentially trip us up (I go into more depth on this in *Did the Devil Make Me Do It?* pages 48-50, commenting on the parallel passage in Matthew 12:43-45), the broad contours of Jesus' teaching lead us to a clear point. He describes a scenario where a demon has been cast out of a person and then proceeds to wander around in the desert before going back to the man. Finding the man's life "swept clean and put in order," he brings seven other spirits with him and makes the man's life worse than it was in the beginning.

The point is that there is no such thing as a spiritual vacuum. If you do nothing, you will be under the influence of the devil. There are no spiritual orphans: either God is your Father or Satan is your master. And so there can be no neutrality or split loyalties in the conflict between Jesus and the devil. Have you thrown your lot in with Christ? If not, do not imagine that you are somehow Switzerland in this cosmic war.

And if you have thrown your lot in with the stronger man, then you must realize that you live your daily life in enemy territory. The world does not share your loyalty to Christ and it does not care about the good of your soul; its default setting is animosity to the things of the Lord. While all people are made in God's image and are thus capable of doing all kinds of good things, their fundamental loyalties are different than yours. And so you must be prepared to walk cautiously in the world.

See To It, Then

How do we do that? Jesus again addresses those who might want to delay making a commitment to him: "No one lights a lamp and puts it in a place where it will be hidden, or under a bowl. Instead they put it on its stand, so that those who come in may see the light" (Luke **11:33**). This is a direct rebuke to those who claim to need a sign before they can commit to Jesus. Their problem is not a lack of information, for Jesus has not hidden his light but shed it abroad.

Instead, the problem is with their eyesight, spiritually speaking. If your spiritual eyes are healthy, your world will be full of light. If your spiritual eyes do not work, your world will be full of darkness (**v 34**). As Edwards puts it,

> "A sound eye … allows the kingdom of God inaugurated by Jesus
> to enter and infuse one's life. People who are receptive to the
> kingdom are thus given light and guidance necessary to negoti-
> ate a dark world." (*The Gospel According to Luke*, page 352)

The key to living in a way that is consistent with the kingdom of God—the key to being for Jesus and not against him—is to have good spiritual vision. If we have it, we will be full of light; if we don't, Jesus says we will be full of darkness. If we see the things of the world as more precious than the things of the kingdom, then we will be in darkness but all the while thinking we have light (**v 35**).

And so the most important question is: how do you get good spiritual eyesight? If that's the key to having a life full of light (**v 36**), then we need to know how to get it. It requires our effort, for Jesus tells us to "see to it" that the light in us is not darkness (**v 35**). And we can be sure that we will not get this eyesight from the wider world, because those who are not with Jesus are against him.

Instead, one of the best ways to develop our spiritual sight is to spend time with other people who love Jesus. They are the ones from whom you will learn kingdom priorities and values. That is not to say that you should seal yourself off hermetically from non-be-lievers, but you should not neglect regular times of fellowship with God's people, for that is one of the ways that God has established for us to improve our sight. As we hear God's word preached regu-larly and work it out in obedience together with other brothers and sisters in our church (**v 28**), we find our eyesight sharpened and the light within us stronger.

Questions for reflection

1. There is no middle ground. Whose side are you on?

2. There is no middle ground. How does that shape the way you see the world around you?

3. How can you make sure you "see to it" that you have healthy spiritual eyesight this week?

12. WOES, WORRIES, AND THE GOSPEL OF FEAR

After Jesus' stinging indictment of the crowd, it is perhaps surprising that he was invited to dine with a Pharisee (**v 37**). But it is not long before a new conflict arises, this time over Jesus' failure to wash his hands before eating (**v 38**). The issue at hand(!) is not hygiene, but rather, the ceremonial washing that the Pharisees so cherished as a sign of ritual cleanness before the Lord. These washing rituals were not required by the Old Testament law, but were a normal part of Jewish tradition.

While we might not understand why anyone would be upset about these kinds of things (see the dust-up described in Mark 7:1-5), Bock explains the situation well:

"This is no neutral matter for the Pharisee or for Jesus, given what it signifies for both. For the Pharisees, the issue is ritual purity before God; for Jesus, it is the additional burdens to God's revelation." (*Luke 9:51–24:53*, page 1112)

While the Pharisee was shocked by Jesus' disregard for the customary washings, Jesus saw what might be an innocuous religious practice as a symbol of everything that was wrong with the Pharisees. Their obsession with washings was an exercise in missing the point akin to merely washing "the outside of the cup and dish" (Luke **11:39**). While there may be nothing wrong with the exterior of a bowl, cleaning it it is a meaningless exercise if the inside is filthy. Such a dish might look fine while it sits on the shelf, but closer examination would reveal that it was not suitable for any significant purpose.

In the same way, the Pharisees' religious rituals amounted to an exercise in missing the point. They obsessed over the external aspects of religious life that could be observed by others ("everything they do is done for people to see," Matthew 23:5-7), but gave little heed to the more unseen and internal aspects of godliness. On the outside, they gave every impression of being righteous. But on the inside, they were "full of greed and wickedness" (Luke **11:39**).

The problem was that the Pharisees did not appreciate God's concern for their hearts. Jesus calls them "foolish people" for failing to understand that the same God who made their "outside" made their "inside" also (**v 40**). This was hardly a new problem; the Old Testament prophets had indicted Israel for their reliance on "human rules" (e.g. Isaiah 29:13) and religious rituals (e.g. Hosea 6:6) in the place of heartfelt love for God and others. Jesus challenged the Pharisees to clean the interior of their cup by exchanging their heart of greed for a spirit of generosity to the poor. Because true holiness begins in the heart, such a change would mean that "everything will be clean" (Luke **11:41**) for them.

Woe There, Pharisees

Jesus then launches into a series of condemnations, beginning with three for the Pharisees. First, they are condemned for giving a tenth of their "mint, rue and all other kinds of garden herbs" (**v 42**). The Old Testament law instructed the people of Israel to set aside a tenth of their produce in order to provide for both the priesthood and the financially vulnerable (Deuteronomy 14:28-29), and Jesus' list of items that the Pharisees gave seems to indicate that they went over and above what the law required. On the face of it this kind of tithing was a good thing—something that they were right not to neglect.

Do not miss what Jesus is saying here. At first glance, the Pharisees' approach to their wealth seemed very godly; most pastors would be happy to have a church full of people who gave as liberally as the Pharisees. But we already know that their hearts were full of greed (Luke **11:39**) and that they lacked generosity towards the poor (**v 41**). Good deeds done from impure motives, in this case a craving for the respect and admiration of others, bring God's condemnation. They should have given their gifts from a heart compelled by love for God and a desire for justice.

The second woe builds on that same theme: "You love the most important seats in the synagogues and respectful greetings in the marketplaces" (**v 43**). The temptation to live for the approval and respect of

> The temptation to live for the respect of others is common to all, but is perhaps especially potent for religious leaders.

other people is common to all people, but is perhaps especially potent for those who are positioned as religious leaders. The Pharisees used their teaching ministry to gain for themselves the most important and honored places in society. But true religion is practiced before the eyes of the Lord and for his approval alone; those who do their deeds of righteousness in order to gain human recognition will receive no further reward from the Lord (see Matthew 6:1).

The third woe could hardly be more pointed or offensive: "You are like unmarked graves, which people walk over without knowing it" (Luke **11:44**). Because contact with a dead body would render a person unclean, graves had to be clearly marked so that people could avoid them. Here Jesus is comparing the Pharisees' corrupt spirituality to something repulsive and full of decay. But even worse than that, he is saying that they have the effect of making unclean those who wander into contact with them. "You travel over land and sea to win a single convert, and when you have succeeded, you make them twice as much a child of hell as you are" (Matthew 23:15).

Woe There, Lawyers

Jesus seems to be on a roll at this point, and anyone with any sense would have stayed out of his way. But religious pride makes people say crazy things and, sure enough, an expert in the law decided to confront Jesus about what he was saying (Luke **11:45**). The "experts in the law," sometimes referred to as "scribes" or "lawyers," were also part of the religious elite of Israel. They were known for their mastery of the Old Testament law, and as such they were among the most respected people in the nation.

While the unnamed expert makes a show of respect to Jesus, calling him "teacher" (**v 45**), his complaint shows that he has not understood anything that Jesus has said. When he objects that Jesus has insulted him and his, he is doing more than merely raising a petulant complaint about hurt feelings. With mind-boggling irony, he is really accusing Jesus of arrogance and haughtiness, which the Old Testament repeatedly condemned (see Psalm 94:2).

Jesus' does not entertain the rebuke for even a moment. He among all of humanity was the only person who never had cause for self-doubt or personal recrimination. He spoke as only a man with a perfectly clear conscience could speak, heaping three more woes for the lawyers on top of what he had already said about the Pharisees.

First, he condemns them because they would "load people down with burdens they can hardly carry" (Luke **11:46**). The law of God was meant to be a blessing and a source of joy and delight to God's people (e.g. Psalm 119:1-16). It was meant to be a way to live out one's love for the Lord, but the scribes had made it into something that paralyzed people with extra rules that went beyond the requirements of God. Instead of helping people to understand and live out the blessings of the law, these experts would "not lift one finger to help them."

The second woe calls up the image of a grave again. Jesus points out that the scribes took it upon themselves to "build tombs for the prophets" (Luke **11:47**) in an **ostentatious** show of piety, but Jesus points out that their forefathers were the reason that the prophets needed to be buried in the first place: "It was your ancestors who killed them." They may have paid lip service to honoring the prophets, but their failure to heed the message of the prophets showed that in reality they stood in solidarity with their ancestors (**v 48**).

It was God's plan that his messengers would be universally rejected or killed (**v 49**). As a result, every generation is in a sense guilty of the violence done against God's messengers by previous generations. As long as they stand in fundamental rejection of those sent to them by the Lord, they will be "held responsible for the blood of all the prophets that has been shed since the beginning of the world" (**v 50**). Not all generations have had the opportunity to kill a prophet, but all generations that have rejected God make it clear that they would do so if they had the opportunity. **Abel** (**v 51**—see Genesis 4:1-16) is the first example of this kind of violence in the Bible, while the stoning of Zechariah (see 2 Chronicles 24:20-21) is the final instance of it in the Old Testament (note that Chronicles was the final book in the Hebrew Bible). From beginning to end, wicked people are out to kill God's messengers.

The third woe (Luke **11:52**) relates to their expertise in the law. God's word was meant to be like a key that opened the door to a blessed relationship with him. But through their teaching, the scribes had made this key inaccessible. They did not use it themselves to enter into a walk with the Lord, and they even made it more difficult for those who were seeking to enter.

One would hope that Jesus' laser-like indictment of their sins against God would have led the religious authorities to remorse and repentance. But once the dinner was complete and Jesus went outside, "the Pharisees and the teachers of the law began to oppose him fiercely and to besiege him with questions, waiting to catch him in something he might say" (**v 53-54**). It is almost as if they were going out of their way to prove and demonstrate the truth of Jesus' observations about their guilt.

Beware Hypocrisy!

We may be tempted to read Jesus' condemnation of the Pharisees and experts in the law and think that it does not have much to say to us. But even though he was surrounded by thousands of people, Jesus wanted to make sure that his disciples understood how this applied to them. He warned them not to follow the path that led to woe, and he went right to the heart of the matter: "Be on your guard against the yeast of the Pharisees, which is hypocrisy" (**12:1**). The heart of the Pharisees' sin was hypocrisy; they presented an external picture that did not match their internal reality. They polished the outside of the cup while the inside was filthy.

But this was a most urgent matter, because their hypocrisy had the properties of yeast. Yeast expands and infiltrates and pervades; it spreads throughout a lump of dough and affects the whole. In the same way, religious hypocrisy has a tendency to recruit others into its charade. When we see others publicly broadcasting their religious performance and their version of obeying God's law (whether or not it is genuine), it is easy to feel pressure to display a similar degree of accomplishment even if it is not backed up by an internal and private reality. Hypocrisy puts the bar at an impossible height and then encourages everyone to pretend that they are jumping over it.

> Religious hypocrisy has a tendency to recruit others into its charade.

Even though there are no longer any Pharisees, their yeast remains a spiritual threat. Whenever Christians are tempted to pretend to be more holy than they are, whenever we are unwilling to confess sin and ask for help, whenever we establish our own man-made rules as the standard for everyone's holiness, whenever we are comfortable with private sins so long as they do not come to light—in those situations the yeast of the Pharisees is present.

If you see something of yourself in the Pharisees (and if you do not, go back and look in the mirror a little more closely!), take note of Jesus' solution to hypocrisy in **verses 2-3**. Hypocrisy depends on the notion that we can hide the truth about ourselves. When someone professes to be godly but indulges their lusts or rage or greed in private, they are operating as if their public persona is the "real" version of themselves. That person is depending on the hope that there is no way that the truth about them could ever be exposed.

Jesus explodes that foundation here. Every "secret" word and deed is open and exposed before the Lord who judges all (see Hebrews 4:13). Whatever our lips might say, the Lord knows what our hearts love. Whatever others see us do, the Lord knows all of our deeds. An awareness of that fact is a powerful antidote to the yeast of the Pharisees that threatens to spread in our hearts.

The 19th-century bishop J.C. Ryle reflected on the implications of God's ability to see and know everything about us, and it's a suitable, and challenging, note on which to end this section:

"How little is this really felt! How many things are done continually, which men would never do if they thought they were seen! How many matters are transacted in the rooms of imagination, which would never bear the light of day! Yes; men entertain thoughts in private, and say words in private, and do acts in private, which they would be ashamed and blush to have exposed before the world. The sound of a footstep coming has stopped many a deed of wickedness. A knock at the door has caused many an evil work to be hastily suspended, and hurriedly laid aside. But oh, what miserable folly is all this! There is an all-seeing Witness with us wherever we go. Lock the door, pull down the blind, turn out the light; it doesn't matter, it makes no difference; God is everywhere, you cannot shut him out, or prevent his seeing." (*The Upper Room*, pages 413-414)

Questions for reflection

1. Have you experienced the "yeast" of religious hypocrisy, either working within or around you? Why is such hypocrisy so attractive, do you think?

2. What would be the easiest way for you to live as a religious hypocrite?

3. How does it make you feel that "there is nothing concealed that will not be disclosed (v 2)? Where in you life does this truth motivate you towards obedience? How does it make you grateful for forgiveness?

PART TWO

All of us know what it is to be afraid. Many of us know what it is to live in fear of something, or someone, for a sustained season, perhaps even our whole lives. Fear is an unproductive feeling—unless there really is something we ought to be afraid of, when we are faced with danger. Christians in many places around the world must deal with people who want to kill their bodies (as in Luke **12:4**). Christians living as a witness in a neighborhood overrun by gangs, or believers in a totalitarian state, or in a region likely to be targeted by terrorists all have reasons to be afraid.

Whom to Fear

But there is something even more frightening than being killed by a terrorist: the certain prospect of our deeds being exposed and brought into judgment (**v 2-3**). In light of that, Jesus tells us that we should fear the God who will give us the justice that we deserve for our sins: "Fear him who, after your body has been killed, has authority to throw you into hell. Yes, I tell you, fear him" (**v 5**). You will one day die and face a God who has the absolute and final authority to send you to eternal punishment for your sins and misdeeds. If you were searching for something to be worried about, that would be a good candidate.

Many Christians do not like to talk about hell anymore, for it seems like the **vestige** of old-time religion. In our therapeutic era, where self-esteem and self-acceptance are the hallmarks of emotional health, the idea that God would find us worthy of punishment must be dangerous and unhealthy—the kind of thing we need to leave in the past. But here we see that Jesus doesn't share that opinion.

According to Jesus, we should be afraid. We should allow this coming reality to occupy our thoughts and minds. And so if you want to know what to fear, fear getting to the end of your life and finding out that you are on the wrong side of God's judgment. This fear enables us to acknowledge Jesus before others (**v 8**), even if such a confession costs us our lives. But if the reality of God's judgment does not compel us and we disown Jesus before others, we will find ourselves disowned by God in the heavenly realms (**v 9**).

These verses lay out a tension that we still feel in our lives. The world can be a scary place for a believer, but only in a provisional way. The world can kill your body, but not your soul. When we are called on to testify to Jesus in a hostile environment, we don't need to be anxious because the Spirit will help us (**v 11**). That doesn't necessarily mean that we won't be killed for our faith, but it does mean that God will help us testify truly and in so doing will preserve our souls. In a sense, the fear of God's judgment is a key to never experiencing God's judgment.

Jesus also warns his hearers against a sin that God will not forgive: "And everyone who speaks a word against the Son of Man will be forgiven, but anyone who blasphemes against the Holy Spirit will not be forgiven" (**v 10**). Much ink has been spilt arguing over the exact meaning of these words, and in the end it may be easier to say what Jesus does *not* mean by his statement. It cannot be that Jesus is teaching that there is a sin that is too great to be covered by his atoning sacrifice (see 1 John 1: 9-10). It also cannot be that God is unwilling to forgive someone who consciously chooses to reject Jesus (or else Peter could never be forgiven for his denial—see Luke 23:54-62).

Instead, it seems best to understand what Jesus is saying as a way of warning us against a persistent rejection of the Spirit's witness to Jesus (referred to in **12:12**). If the ministry of the Spirit is bound up in witnessing to God's salvation in the person of Christ, then to obstinately judge that witness as false necessarily puts one outside of that salvation. Someone who desires forgiveness through faith in Jesus cannot be guilty of this sin. Graham Cole sums up the biblical evidence well:

> "Blasphemy against the Holy Spirit is that self-righteous persistent refusal to embrace the offer of salvation in Christ: his ministry of restoring his Father's broken creation. It is to set one's face

against the Spirit's testimony to Christ as the Son of Man with the authority to forgive sins. The problem is the human heart settled in opposition to God. Without repentance there is no forgiveness." (*Engaging with the Holy Spirit*, page 29)

A Frightening Story

The parable that follows in **verses 13-21** illustrates in miniature what Jesus has been talking about. The context for the story is that a man came to Jesus for help with a family dispute regarding an inheritance (**v 13**). In a bit of irony, the one to whom the Father has given all judgment wonders why this man would come to him for resolution of such a squabble (**v 14**). Instead of resolving the conflict, Jesus told a parable that addressed a far more weighty matter.

The story itself (**v 16-19**) is a fairly simple one. A fertile field makes a rich man even richer. After some shrewd investments in infrastructure, he looks forward to sitting back and saying to himself, "You have plenty of grain laid up for many years. Take life easy; eat, drink and be merry" (**v 19**). But there is a catch, for that very night he is to die and give an account for his life (**v 20**). In the end, such a man is a fool; he did not worry about the most important thing: being rich toward God (**v 21**). When it came time for him to give an account for his life, he was materially wealthy but spiritually destitute.

The parable refocuses the attention of the person who wants help with his inheritance. He might have a legal case, but the greater concern is for the hold that money might have on his heart. Using him as an example, Jesus warns the crowd to, "Watch out! Be on your guard against all kinds of greed; life does not consist in an abundance of possessions" (**v 15**, see **v 23**). The foolish rich man illustrates the point; he had the abundance of possessions that the man in the crowd hoped would one day be his through the disputed inheritance, but he did not have true spiritual life. And so we must be on guard against the deceitfulness of riches that would cause us to fear a dip in the stock market more than we fear our Creator and Judge. Wealth tempts us to trust in it, but when all of the secrets of our hearts are disclosed, our money will not be able to protect us from God's judgment.

Why We Needn't Fear

As the parable points out, the problem with many of us is that we fear the wrong things. And while the prospect of divine judgment might not seem like a positive thing, in reality the fear of the Lord frees us from all the other fears that plague our day-to-day lives. If you have got the fear of God right, then you don't need to fear anything else.

In a world like ours, Jesus' words are like a shimmering oasis in the desert: *Don't fear.* He tells his followers not to fear the violence that other people might do to them (**v 4**). He tells them not to be anxious when they are called upon to defend themselves before hostile authorities (**v 11**). And he tells them not to worry about physical necessities like food and drink and clothing (**v 22** and **v 29**).

It is all well and good for someone to tell you not to be afraid. But fears do not subside without a good reason, and so what we really need is to know is why we are really safe. To that end, Jesus gives three basic reasons why we should not be afraid.

First, there is a wonderfully practical reason: "Who of you by worrying can add a single hour to your life? Since you cannot do this very little thing, why do you worry about the rest?" (**v 25-26**). It turns out that anxiety is incredibly inefficient; it consumes a lot of resources but accomplishes nothing of importance. The next time you begin to obsess over the things you fear, simply heed Jesus' warning that it does not help; it is a dead-end street.

But even more importantly, Jesus tells us not to fear because God has promised to help his people. He tells his followers that in the moment of crisis the Holy Spirit will teach them what they need to know and say (**v 12**). God is committed to his people, and so he will make sure that "these things [that is, the things that we need] will be given to you as well" (**v 31**). In the end, what more could you want? People who do not know God are worried and anxious (**v 30**); that makes sense. But if God is so intimately involved in our lives that he knows the number of hairs on our heads (**v 7**) and knows everything that we need (**v 30**), what sense does it make to live in fear?

And most importantly, the third reason why we shouldn't fear is that God loves us. In this passage, Jesus makes some arguments from the lesser to the greater. If God cares for sparrows (**v 6-7**) and ravens (**v 24**) and clothes the flowers in the field (**v 27-28**), how much more will he provide for all that you need. The point is that you are infinitely more valuable to God than a bird (**v 24**), so you can trust his loving provision for you. In the end, if a powerful and loving God has declared his intention to take care of you, there is nothing to be afraid of. No economic shift or political change or even our own folly and failure can frustrate God's purposes.

> If a powerful, loving God has declared his intention to take care of you, there is nothing to be afraid of.

This does not mean that we will not know troubles and loss. But notice that Jesus does not say, *Do not fear, for everything will always go the way you want it to go.* He does not even tell us what the future will hold; otherwise we could manage our expectations and figure things out on our own. Instead, what we get is something better: the promise that God knows what we need and loves us. Jesus tenderly urges his "little flock" to "not be afraid" (**v 32**). God's loving care is a safe place in which to locate your hope and confidence.

In the end, your fear reveals a lot about your theology. When you embrace anxiety and worry, you are embracing a set of beliefs about God, his love for you, and his ability to take care of you. The Bible actually has a category for faithful anxiety (e.g. 2 Corinthians 11:28;

1 Corinthians 7:32-34): a passionate concern for good that doesn't spiral into fear and bitterness, but rather, leads us to pray and trust in the Lord, giving thanks for what we do have even as we cry out to him about what we do not (Philippians 4:6-8). But when our anxiety is fueled by fear, the Bible talks about it less in terms of a weakness of constitution that needs to be overcome, and more as a sin to be avoided and repented of (1 Peter 5:5-7).

The Gospel of Fear

If we take seriously what Jesus is saying in this passage, it will create some tension in our minds. On one hand, Jesus tells us to be afraid of God because he can throw us into hell; God is holy and hates sin. On the other hand, Jesus encourages us to look to our merciful heavenly Father in trust for all that we need. How can we reconcile those two things?

Ultimately, they can only be reconciled at the cross of Christ. At the cross, God poured out his holy wrath on Jesus instead of pouring it out on his people. There we see a God who is righteous and justly angry about our sin. This is a God to fear. But at the cross we also see the love of God on display most clearly. There we see a God who loved his "little flock" so much that he sent his only Son to take their punishment. This awfully holy God is more lovingly disposed toward us than we could ever fathom. That truth should set us free from the crippling fears that enslave those who do not know this God (Luke **12:30**). He has set us free in order that we might seek his kingdom with our whole lives (**v 31**) and then show the world how glorious and loving and trustworthy God is.

The great 18th-century pastor Jonathan Edwards was once fired (wrongly) by the congregation that he had served faithfully for some time. In addition to the humiliation and financial troubles that came with his dismissal, he also had to endure being harshly criticized and attacked by people that he had loved. In those circumstances, any person would be tempted to give in to fear and anxiety. But one observer recorded in his journal that Edwards was able to remain peaceful throughout:

> "I never saw the least symptoms of displeasure in his **countenance** the whole week, but he appeared like a man of God, *whose happiness was out of the reach of his enemies* and whose treasure was not only a future but a present good, overbalancing all imaginable ills of life..."
>
> (Quoted in Marsden, *Jonathan Edwards: A Life*, page 361: italics mine)

When we locate it in our holy and loving God, our happiness can always be out of the reach of anything that would seek to harm us.

We see in Jesus' words a reminder of the way that Luke's Gospel began. Zechariah (1:12-14), Mary (1:29-30) and the shepherds (2:9-10) all heard their angelic visitors speak a word of joy and comfort to them in their fear. It was sensible to be afraid in the presence of one of God's angels (1:19), but these messengers were sent with news of great joy. Here in chapter 12, we hear an echo of that pattern: the good news of Jesus is that God is a frightening judge, but he has shown great love and care for us in Christ. When we trust him, he replaces our anxiety with peace and our fear with joy. The King has come. He came to bring the joy of his presence and his salvation. Fear not!

Questions for reflection

1. All through Luke's Gospel, we've seen that the emotional marker of faith is joy. How are you experiencing this in your own life?

2. What do you most worry about? Are those worries sapping you of joy?

3. How has this passage given you reason not to worry in those ways? How will you go about putting this into practice in your thinking, praying and living?

GLOSSARY

Abel: Adam and Eve's son. When God accepted Abel's offering and not his brother Cain's, Cain killed his brother (see Genesis 4:1-16).

Abraham: the ancestor of the nation of Israel, and the man God made a binding agreement (covenant) with. God promised to make his family into a great nation, give them a land, and bring blessing to all nations through one of his descendants (see Genesis 12:1-3).

Agnostic: unsure about something, on the basis that there is not enough evidence.

Ambivalence: mixed feelings.

Apostle: one of the men appointed directly by the risen Christ to teach about him with authority.

Ascetic: someone who refrains from fun and pleasure for religious reasons.

Autonomy: the ability to make our own decisions without being directed by anyone else; to be self-governing.

Barometers: an instrument used to measure atmospheric pressure, which in turn can predict what the weather will be.

Blasphemy: disrespecting or mocking God.

Blessed: to be in right relationship with God, enjoying his love and favor.

Caesar Augustus: the first Roman emperor, from 27 BC – AD 14.

Calvary: the place on the outskirts of Jerusalem where Jesus was crucified.

Canaanite: of the land or people of Canaan (i.e. those who lived among, or around, the nation of Israel). Canaanites did not worship the God of Israel.

Censorious: very critical of others.

Circumcision: God told the men among his people in the Old Testament to be circumcised as a way to show physically that they knew and trusted him, and belonged to the people of God (see Genesis 17).

Connote: imply or suggest.

Countenance: face.

Covenant: a binding agreement between two parties. God had made a covenant with the people of Israel, sometimes known as the **Old Covenant**.

Cult: a religious community that exercises excessive and unhealthy power over its members.

Demoniac: someone possessed by a demon.

Demurred: showed reluctance.

Diabolic: something that is from, or inspired by, the devil. A **diabolic counterfeit** is a fake or fraud inspired by/provided by the devil.

Discipleship: following Jesus as Lord and trusting him as Savior.

Elijah: an Old Testament prophet who announced God's judgment for his people's idolatry.

Elisha: an Old Testament prophet and Elijah's successor.

Emphatic: said in a forceful way.

Empirically: able to be seen or observed.

Enigmatic: mysterious; hard to understand.

Euphemism: an indirect way of saying something else.

Evangelicals: Christians who, broadly speaking, emphasize the importance of personal conversion through faith in Christ, and the authority of the Bible.

Eviscerate: remove the internal organs of a slaughtered animal.

Exaltation: when Jesus ascended into heaven and was given glory and authority by the Father (see Philippians 2:9).

Exorcisms: casting out an evil spirit from a person who appears to be possessed.

Fallen: affected by God's judgment, which was a consequence of the fall—the event when the first man and woman disobeyed God (see Genesis 3).

Fermentation: the process in which yeast or bacteria is used to make drink alcoholic.

Finite: limited; mortal.

Franciscans: a religious order of monks.

Galilean: someone from the region of Galilee, in the north of first-century Israel.

Gentiles: people who are not ethnically Jewish.

Gospel: 1. One of the four historical records of Jesus found in the New Testament—written by Matthew, Mark, Luke, and John. 2. An announcement, often translated "good news." When the Roman Emperor sent a proclamation around the empire declaring a victory or achievement, this was called a "gospel." The gospel is good news to be believed, not good advice to be followed.

Grace: unmerited favor. In the Bible, "grace" is usually used to describe how God treats his people. Because God is full of grace, he gives believers eternal life (see Ephesians 2:4-8); he also gives them gifts to use to serve his people (see Ephesians 4:7, 11-13).

Gynaecological: relating to the female reproductive system.

Hannah: the mother of the prophet Samuel. She was previously infertile but prayed to the Lord for a child and he granted her Samuel.

Heathen: here meaning non-Jewish.

Hermit: a person who lives alone in isolation for religious reasons.

Hypocrisy: when what one says and what one does do not match up.

Idolatry: serving and worshiping something other than the true God as the source of blessing and security.

Illocutionary: what is actually meant by what is said. For example, if one asks, "Is there any black pepper?" the illocutionary effect—the actual meaning—is "Give me some black pepper."

Implicitly: suggests indirectly.

Impudence: disrespect.

Inaugurated: formally begun; brought in.

Incarnation: the coming of the divine Son of God as a human, in the person of Jesus Christ.

Incredulity: being unwilling to believe something.

Inordinately: excessively; disproportionately.

Itinerant: travelling from place to place.

Jettison: abandon, discard.

King David: the second King of Israel, whose reign was the high-point of Israel's history. God promised that one of David's descendants would reign forever—the Messiah (see 2 Samuel 7).

Kingdom (of God): in this instance meaning life under Jesus Christ's perfect rule. We enter God's kingdom when we turn to his Son, Jesus, in repentance and faith; we will enjoy the kingdom fully when Jesus returns to this world and establishes his kingdom over the whole earth.

Malachi: the final Old Testament prophet, who said that the day of the Lord was coming, hailed by one who looked like Elijah.

Manna: the "bread" that God miraculously provided each morning for the Israelites to eat while they were journeying to the promised land (see Exodus 16). It looked like white flakes.

Martyrs: people who die for their beliefs or cause.

Mediator: someone who brings two enemies together and makes it possible for them to be friends again.

Medium: the means by which a message is delivered, e.g. in writing, by telephone.

Megalomaniacal: obsessed with power.

Messiah: see pages 125-126.

Metaphor: an image which is used to explain something, but which is not to be taken literally (e.g. "The news was a dagger to his heart").

Minor key: a musical term; music that sounds sad is usually in a minor key (as opposed to a major key).

Mutually exclusive: two things or opinions that cannot both be true, or exist, at the same time. E.g. "Jesus is God." "Jesus is not divine."

Noxious: poisonous.

Obsolete: no longer useful.

Orthodox: standard, accepted teaching.

Ostentatious: showy.

Pagans: people who don't know and worship the true God.

Parables: memorable stories told to illustrate a truth about Jesus and/ or his kingdom.

Paradigm: a model or pattern.

Paradoxical: describing two true statements that seem to be contradictory, but aren't.

Passover: the event recorded in the book of Exodus, when God rescued his people from slavery in Egypt through sending plagues, the final one of which was the death of the firstborn in every family, which could be avoided only by killing a lamb in the firstborn's place so that God's judgment would "pass over" that household (see Exodus 12 – 13).

Pentecost: a Jewish feast celebrating God giving his people his law on Mount Sinai (Exodus 19 – 31). On the day of this feast, fifty days after Jesus' resurrection, the Holy Spirit came to the first Christians (Acts 2), so "Pentecost" is how Christians tend to refer to this event.

Periphery: edge.

Pharisee: leaders of a first-century Jewish sect who were extremely strict about keeping God's laws, and who added extra laws around God's law to ensure that they wouldn't break it. They tended to focus on external acts of obedience.

Piety: religious good deeds. Someone who prioritizes such deeds is **pious**.

Porcine: relating to pigs.

Provisional: only for now; limited.

Quirinius: Roman governor over what is now Syria, from AD 6 – 12.

Rabbi: a Jewish religious teacher.

Rectitude: morally correct.

Redemption: the act of freeing or releasing someone (in this case, from slavery to sin); buying someone back for a price.

Religious establishment: the group in charge of religious practices and rituals.

Righteous: the status of being in a right relationship with God.

Sabbath: Saturday; the holy day when Jewish people were commanded not to work (see Exodus 20:8-11).

Samaritans: people from the region of Samaria; a people group with mixed Jewish-pagan ancestry and religion.

Scientific era: our modern era, in which scientific knowledge is more highly prized than other forms, including religious tradition.

Sodom, Tyre and Sidon: Sodom was a city that was destroyed by God as punishment for its wickedness (Genesis 19). Tyre and Sidon were Gentile cities north of Galilee, that Jesus never went to.

Sovereign: royal, all-powerful.

Submission: voluntarily accepting the will of another.

Symphony: a beautiful and complicated piece of music played by an orchestra.

Temporal realm: the current, earthly realm, as opposed to the eternal realm.

Tetrarch: the ruler or governor of one of four divisions of a Roman province.

Theological: focusing on God's perspective and the truth about him.

Trajectory: path, course or pattern.

Transcendent: far above what is humanly possible.

Trials: difficult or testing periods of life; e.g. a time of ill-health, or persecution, or loneliness, or unemployment.

Trinity: the biblical doctrine that the one God is three Persons, distinct from one another, each fully God, of the same "essence" (or "God-ness"). We usually call these three Persons Father, Son and Holy Spirit.

Twelve tribes of Israel: the twelve communities that made up the Old Testament people of Israel. Each tribe was descended from the son of Jacob, after whom they were named (see Genesis 49:1-28).

Vengeance: punishment for wrongdoing.

Verbatim: in words that are exactly the same as the original ones.

Vestige: trace, remnant.

Vindication: being cleared of suspicion and proved to have been right.

Visceral: a response or decision that comes from strong emotions, and not from logic or reason.

Vocational missionaries: people whose full-time job is telling people about Jesus, usually in a nation or culture that is not their own.

Winnowing: the process of removing the edible grain from the inedible husks it grows in.

Works-based religion: the view that a person's good works (i.e. thoughts, words and actions) can save them.

Wrath: God's settled, deserved hatred of and anger at sin.

Zealous: to be extremely passionate, enthusiastic and uncompromising about something.

BIBLIOGRAPHY

- C.D. Agan, *The Imitation of Christ in the Gospel of Luke: Growing in Christlike Love for God and Neighbor* (P&R, 2014)

- Jonathan Aitken, *John Newton: From Disgrace to Amazing Grace* (Crossway, 2013)

- G.K. Beale and D.A Carson, *Commentary on the New Testament Use of the Old Testament* (Baker Academic, 2007)

- Darrell L. Bock, *Luke 1:1 – 9:50* in the Baker Exegetical Commentary on the New Testament Series (Baker Academic, 1994)

- Darrell L. Bock, *Luke 9:51 – 24:53* in the Baker Exegetical Commentary on the New Testament Series (Baker Academic, 1994)

- Graham Cole, *Engaging with the Holy Spirit: Real Questions, Practical Answers* (Crossway, 2008)

- James R. Edwards, *The Gospel According to Luke* in The Pillar New Testament Commentary Series (Eerdmans, 2015)

- Joel B. Green, *The Gospel of Luke* in The New International Commentary on the New Testament Series (Eerdmans, 1997)

- Timothy Keller, *Generous Justice* (Dutton, 2010)

- J. Gresham Machen, *The Virgin Birth of Christ* (Baker, 1974)

- George M. Marsden, *Jonathan Edwards: A Life* (Yale University Press, 2003)

- Mike McKinley, *Did the Devil Make Me Do It?* (The Good Book Company, 2013)

- J.C. Ryle, *The Upper Room: Biblical Truths for Modern Times* (The Banner of Truth, 2006)

■ Huston Smith, *The Religions of Man* (Harper & Row, 1958)

■ Kline R. Snodgrass, *Stories With Intent* (Eerdmans, 2008)

■ R.C. Sproul, *The Holiness of God* (Tyndale, 1998)

■ John R.W. Stott, *The Cross of Christ* (IVP, 1986)

■ Paul David Tripp, *Instruments in the Redeemer's Hands* (P&R, 2002)

■ Virgil, *The Aeneid,* translated A.S. Kline (CreateSpace, 2014)

■ B.B. Warfield, *The Person and Work of Christ* (Benediction Classics, 2015)

Luke for...
Bible-study Groups

Mike McKinley's **Good Book Guide** to Luke 1–12 is the companion to this resource, helping groups of Christians to explore, discuss and apply Luke's Gospel together. Eight studies, each including investigation, apply, getting personal, pray and explore more sections, take you through the first half of the Gospel. Includes a concise Leader's Guide at the back.

Find out more at:
www.thegoodbook.com/goodbookguides

Daily Devotionals

Explore daily devotional helps you open up the Scriptures and will encourage and equip you in your walk with God. Published as a quarterly booklet, *Explore* is also available as an app, where you can download Mike's notes on Luke, alongside contributions from trusted Bible teachers including Timothy Keller, Mark Dever, Juan Sanchez, Tim Chester and Sam Allberry.

Find out more at:
www.thegoodbook.com/explore

More For You

1 Samuel For You

"As we read this gripping part of Israel's history, we see Jesus Christ with fresh colour and texture. And we see what it means for his people to follow him as King in an age that worships personal freedom."

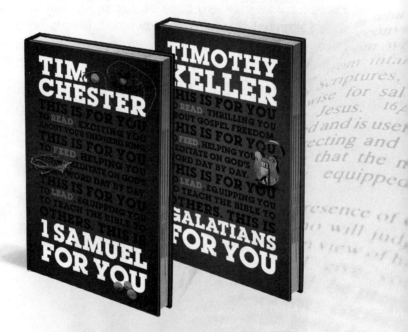

Galatians For You

"The book of Galatians is dynamite. It is an explosion of joy and freedom which leaves us enjoying a deep significance, security and satisfaction. Why? Because it brings us face to face with the gospel—the A to Z of the Christian life."

The Series

Luke 1–12 For You is the twelfth in the *God's Word For You series*. Other titles are:

- **Exodus For You** *Tim Chester*
- **Judges For You** *Timothy Keller*
- **1 Samuel For You** *Tim Chester*
- **Daniel For You** *David Helm*
- **Romans 1 - 7 For You** *Timothy Keller*
- **Romans 8 - 16 For You** *Timothy Keller*
- **Galatians For You** *Timothy Keller*
- **Ephesians For You** *Richard Coekin*
- **Titus For You** *Tim Chester*
- **James For You** *Sam Allberry*
- **1 Peter For You** *Juan Sanchez*

Forthcoming titles include:

- **Micah For You** *Stephen Um*
- **John For You (two volumes)**
  Josh Moody
- **Acts For You (two volumes)**
  Al Mohler
- **Philippians For You** *Steven Lawson*

Find out more about these resources at:
www.thegoodbook.com/for-you

thegoodbook
COMPANY
Opening up the Bible

At The Good Book Company, we are dedicated to helping Christians and local churches grow. We believe that God's growth process always starts with hearing clearly what he has said to us through his timeless word—the Bible.

Ever since we opened our doors in 1991, we have been striving to produce resources that honor God in the way the Bible is used. We have grown to become an international provider of user-friendly resources to the Christian community, with believers of all backgrounds and denominations using our Bible studies, books, evangelistic resources, DVD-based courses and training events.

We want to equip ordinary Christians to live for Christ day by day, and churches to grow in their knowledge of God, their love for one another, and the effectiveness of their outreach.

Call us for a discussion of your needs or visit one of our local websites for more information on the resources and services we provide.

Your friends at The Good Book Company

NORTH AMERICA   thegoodbook.com   866 244 2165
UK & EUROPE thegoodbook.co.uk 0333 123 0880
AUSTRALIA thegoodbook.com.au (02) 6100 4211
NEW ZEALAND thegoodbook.co.nz (+64) 3 343 2463

 WWW.CHRISTIANITYEXPLORED.ORG
Our partner site is a great place for those exploring the Christian faith, with a clear explanation of the good news, powerful testimonies and answers to difficult questions.